"The story of Joseph is one of the most intriguing and instructive found in all the Old Testament. Deception, betrayal, deprivation, and injustice, as well as mercy, forgiveness, providence, and love are all prominently displayed in its telling. Undergirding, permeating, and guiding the events of Joseph's life, however, is the gospel of Jesus Christ. With careful exegesis, theological precision, and pastoral sensitivity, Baucham explains Joseph's story with a freshness that highlights the glorious grace of God in the gospel."

Thomas Ascol, Senior Pastor, Grace Baptist Church of Cape Coral, Florida; Executive Director, Founders Ministries

JOSEPH AND THE GOSPEL OF MANY COLORS

JOSEPH

AND THE GOSPEL OF MANY COLORS

READING AN OLD STORY IN A NEW WAY

VODDIE BAUCHAM JR.

 CROSSWAY

WHEATON, ILLINOIS

Published in association with Yates & Yates, www.yates2.com.

Cover design and image: Brandon Hill Photos

First printing 2013

Printed in the United States of America

Unless otherwise indicated, Scripture quotations are from the ESV® Bible (*The Holy Bible, English Standard Version®*), copyright © 2001 by Crossway. 2011 Text Edition. Used by permission. All rights reserved.

All emphases in Scripture quotations have been added by the author.

Trade paperback ISBN: 978-1-4335-2373-1
PDF ISBN: 978-1-4335-2374-8
Mobipocket ISBN: 978-1-4335-2385-4
ePub ISBN: 978-1-4335-2386-1

Library of Congress Cataloging-in-Publication Data
Baucham, Voddie.
   Joseph and the gospel of many colors : reading an old story in a new way / Voddie Baucham, Jr.
     pages cm
   Includes bibliographical references and index.
   ISBN 978-1-4335-2373-1
   1. Joseph (Son of Jacob) 2. Typology (Theology) 3. Bible.
O.T. Genesis XXXVII-L—Criticism, interpretation, etc.
I. Title.
BS580.J6B38   2013
222'.11092—dc23   2013012666

Crossway is a publishing ministry of Good News Publishers.

VP		23	22	21	20	19	18	17	16	15	14	13
15	14	13	12	11	10	9	8	7	6	5	4	3	2	1

CONTENTS

INTRODUCTION

At first glance, this book may seem incongruent with what I've written in the past. I assure you it is not. This book is firmly rooted in two ideas that have always motivated my ministry and writing. First, this book is rooted in biblical exposition. Like my first two books, *The Ever-Loving Truth* and *Family Driven Faith*, this book is an extended exposition of a specific portion of Scripture. We serve a God who speaks. More specifically, God has spoken to us through his Word. There is no higher pursuit for those of us who love and serve God than to know and proclaim that which he has spoken. This is precisely what *The Gospel of Many Colors* is all about.

Another aspect of this book that is congruent with my previous work is that it was born out of the synergy between church and home. If *Family Shepherds* was a practical expansion of my previous works, then this book is an even more specific and practical expansion of *Family Shepherds*. Here I am answering the question, how do we teach the Bible in practical, meaningful ways? The journey that resulted in this work involved answering that question in both the church and the home.

LET'S PREACH THROUGH GENESIS

First, the leaders of our church decided to teach through Genesis in our pulpit ministry. As Pastor of Preaching, it was my responsibility to do an analysis and overview of the book, divide it into teaching segments, and assign passages among the elders. In preparation for doing so, I read through the book of Genesis again in a single sitting. I was amazed at how much I gleaned just from doing this. I was familiar with the book; I had studied it, read it, quoted from it, even memorized from it. However, it is always eye-opening to read through a book of the Bible from front to back.

We then had to divide the book. This is where things really began to develop. Since Genesis has fifty chapters, we would either have to devote several years to teaching through it or divide it into major segments with intermittent breaks. We chose the latter. We decided on four sections: Genesis 1–11 (creation/cosmology/worldview); Genesis 12–22 (the life of Abraham); Genesis 23–36 (Isaac and Jacob); Genesis 37–50 (the life of Joseph and beyond).

This was the first time I delved deeply into the life of Joseph. Of course, I was familiar with, and thought fondly of, Joseph's character. However, I had never dealt seriously with other questions surrounding this biblical hero. What were the main events in his story? Who were the main characters? What was the main message? These questions and others led me to realize a truth that became the thesis upon which this book is based: the life of Joseph isn't really about Joseph at all! Moses was uncovering something far more significant in this section of the Genesis narrative.

Second, since we were dividing the book into four segments, we planned to leave Genesis intermittently to preach from New Testament books. This led to an unexpected blessing. As we preached through large swaths of the New Testament (for example, the Sermon on the Mount, 1 John, and sections of Romans), it became more and more obvious that (1) Genesis was indeed foundational to biblical theology, systematic theology, and Christian cosmology/worldview; and (2) the New Testament writers had much to offer in terms of interpreting Genesis.

Adam, Noah, and Abraham are mentioned throughout the New Testament, and those mentions are crucial to understanding both the significance *of* the book of Genesis and what is actually significant *in* the book of Genesis. I discovered the paltry number of references to Joseph in the New Testament and found myself asking, "How could such a beloved biblical character be such a minor player in the eyes of the New Testament writers?" Of course, the New Testament writers hadn't missed something, but had I? Had I been guilty of making more of Joseph and his story than the Bible intended?

Finally, in the midst of all of this, I decided to teach through Genesis during our family worship time at home. Each evening we opened the pages of this fascinating book and walked step-by-step through the entire thing. It took us several months, and the results were astounding.

It was this final leg in the journey that helped me put all the pieces together. Here, sitting in front of my children (ranging in age from newborn to late teens), I had to figure out how to present the message of Genesis in ways both simple and profound. I had to answer probing questions from young adults and satisfy the curiosity of little children. Why did Adam eat the fruit? Why did Noah get drunk? Why did Abraham give his wife away? Why did he commit adultery? Why did Isaac love one of his boys more than the other? And on and on!

It didn't take long to realize that the book of Genesis was not just a collection of character studies designed to blaze the paths for seekers of holiness. I couldn't just point to the good characters and say, "Be like him," and to the bad characters and warn, "Don't be like him." They were all flawed and in desperate need of redemption—just like my children and me, and just like my fellow church members and me. And there it was—I not only knew how to approach Genesis in family worship; I knew how to approach it in general. Studying the book of Genesis with my family was the final piece that caused the life of Joseph to come into clear focus. I knew where he fit in the overall structure of the book of Genesis. I knew where he fit in the scope of redemptive history. I knew where he fit in the context of a gospel-centered approach to teaching and preaching, both in the church and in the home.

The next several months were filled with rich, fruitful times of family worship at home and corporate worship at church. My family and I fell in love with the book of Genesis, as did our church family. It was as though someone had turned the lights on and we could all see what had been there all along.

Soon I began to teach on the life of Joseph in other settings. I watched the same thing happen abroad that I had seen at home. People were seeing Joseph, and the book of Genesis, in a new light. Not because of some special revelation or "new teaching" that had come along, but because of what had been there all along. After years and years of moralistic character studies, people found a gospel-centered approach to this familiar narrative refreshing, liberating, and convicting.

WHAT THIS BOOK IS NOT

This is not a book of sermons. I have not collected my sermons on the life of Joseph and edited them into book form. In fact, because of the nature of our church's team teaching model, I didn't have the privilege of preaching all the messages on Joseph. Moreover, much of what has developed into this book came *after* our series on Genesis was completed. Like any preacher who practices systematic exposition will tell you, the time you feel most prepared to start preaching through a book is when you've just finished doing so. It is only then that you are able to see the big picture and the interconnectedness of the text as a whole.

This is not a commentary on Genesis 37–50. My goal here was not to provide technical or scholarly insights on this portion of the Genesis narrative. I lack both the expertise and the inclination to accomplish such a task. I am neither an Old Testament scholar nor a Hebrew expert. Plenty of quality commentaries are out there written by men far more qualified than I, and I commend them to you (see the bibliography).

In fact, you will find that I have not even included many notes from commentaries or other sources. That is by design. My goal was not to present the results of having combed through mountains of material. I want the reader to grasp the significance of a careful reading of the text. This is about observation. This is something we all can and should do.

This book is also not an allegory of the life of Joseph. There is much talk about Christ-centered preaching, and I am glad to see it.

However, the response from many evangelical circles is skepticism. Repeatedly, I have faced questions like, "Does preaching Christ in every passage mean allegorizing the text?" And again, "Aren't you Christ-centered preachers ignoring the grammatical/historical aspects of the text?" Let me say that these are legitimate concerns. Christocentrism done poorly is as bad if not worse than moralism, as antinomianism is no better than legalism.

WHAT THIS BOOK IS

My goal in this book was not to find Christ behind every rock. It was, however, to be mindful of the gospel at every turn. The only character worth exalting in Scripture is the character of Christ. Anything we see in the character of another is only praiseworthy to the degree that it reflects the character of Christ. The Bible is not a book of character studies; it is a book of redemption. Joseph is a link in the chain of redemption. Therefore, reading and interpreting the life of Joseph, if done right, will exalt God's redemptive work. It is my sincere hope that this is precisely what this book does.

1

THE LORD OF THE STORY

Joseph is one of the most beloved characters in the Bible. His story reads like a prime-time special! Jealousy, sibling rivalry, murder plot, betrayal, suffering, deepening despair, apparent deliverance that does not come, all followed by a dramatic turn of events and triumphant ascension. And all that before reunion and restoration! Hollywood wishes it could write stories like that.

Ironically, it is the dramatic nature of Joseph's story, coupled with our addiction to heroic character arcs and story lines, that make it difficult to interpret this well-worn narrative properly. Our tendency is to look at the story in isolation as though it were one of Aesop's fables with a moral at the end: "Let 'em hate you. If you're faithful, you'll end up rich, powerful, and vindicated." However, this interpretation not only misses the mark, it also perverts the very message of the narrative in particular, and the Bible in general. Joseph is not a mere example of what awaits us if we're "good enough." His story, like every story in the Bible, is part of the broader redemptive narrative designed to cause us to recognize the glory of our great God.

A LETTER FROM A JEWESS

I've told this story before, but it bears repeating. My "aha moment" as it relates to preaching the gospel from all of Scripture came about seven years ago when I got a letter from a Jewish woman. This was not an e-mail, a Facebook message, or a Tweet; this was a letter. You know: those things people don't have time to write anymore.

The woman had heard a sermon I preached on an Old Testament passage and was absolutely moved; she was so moved that she felt the need to write me a letter. As I read the letter, I could tell that she was pleasantly surprised by the sermon. As a Conservative Jew, she loved the Bible and was grateful to hear it taught, but she never thought she could get so much out of a message preached by a Gentile.

As I read her letter, my eyes filled with tears. However, these were not tears of joy because the Lord had used my sermon in the life of a Jew. On the contrary, these were tears of horror and shame! As I read her words, all I could think of were Paul's words: "But we preach Christ crucified, a stumbling block to Jews and folly to Gentiles, but to those who are called, both Jews and Greeks, Christ the power of God and the wisdom of God" (1 Cor. 1:23–24). So why wasn't my message a "stumbling block" to this Jew? Was it because she was "being saved"? No. It was because *I had not preached Christ!*

I had preached a verse-by-verse, expository message from an Old Testament passage, but I hadn't preached the gospel. And this was not unusual! I was steeped in an expository tradition that was so concerned with the "historical/grammatical" exegesis of texts that it became "atomistic" in its execution. Not wanting to wander from my text, I would force myself to "dig deep" and serve up the best, richest morsels I could find. If the passage was "evangelistic," my message was evangelistic. If the text was "discipleship" oriented; then so was my message. If the text was about practical matters, I did not want to "spiritualize" it and make it about something else. I wanted to be "true to the text" no matter what.

The result was Christless moralism: sermons that wouldn't even cut to the heart of one who has rejected Christ in favor of the Law, but instead affirmed them in their horrific error. And there I sat holding the evidence in my hands. Something had to change . . . but how? Did I have to give up exposition? Did I have to avoid Old Testament narrative? What was I to do?

The first thing I had to do was come face-to-face with my failure. I had to be honest about what I was doing, and why.

THE MORASS OF MORALISM

In his book *Soul Searching*, Christian Smith identifies the overarching theological perspective plaguing the religious lives of America's young people as "Moralistic, Therapeutic Deism."[1] This belief is characterized by five major tenets. First, there is a God who created the world. Second, God wants us to be good (as is common to all religions). Third, the main goal in life is to be happy and feel good about one's self. Fourth, God does not need to be particularly involved in our lives unless we need something. Fifth, good people go to heaven when they die.[2]

A quick glance at this list reveals that this worldview dominates not only the spiritual lives of teens; this thinking is ubiquitous! As a result, it becomes natural to look at the Bible as no more than a guide to morality. As a preacher, a parent, an American, and a Christian, I fight this same tendency. My church is filled with sinners; I need to preach morality. My children are disobedient; I need to preach morality. America is going to hell in a handbasket; the church hasn't done its job . . . preaching morality. I need to be a better Christian; I need to listen to someone preaching morality. We've replaced the Beatles' famous refrain, "All You Need Is Love" with "All You Need Is Morality."

As a result, we read the Bible in search of morals. Moreover, we become accustomed to—even desirous of—preaching that is moralistic. This, in turn, leads to positive feedback for preachers and teachers who emphasize moralism, which of course leads to more moralistic preaching.

If you are familiar with the story of Joseph at all, you probably think about it in moralistic categories. As a result, you see the utility of the passages in their ability to motivate believers to do better and to show unbelievers the benefits of serving God. And if you're like me, you've rarely, if ever, thought about the gospel-centered/redemptive-historical significance of the narrative. Instead, we tend to be led by several pieces of low-hanging fruit.

The first reason we tend to revert to moralism is the fact that God's law "is holy, and the commandment is holy and righteous and good" (Rom. 7:12). This, however, does not mean that the way we use the law is always good:

> Now we know that the law is good, if one uses it lawfully, understanding this, that the law is not laid down for the just but for the lawless and disobedient, for the ungodly and sinners, for the unholy and profane, for those who strike their fathers and mothers, for murderers, the sexually immoral, men who practice homosexuality, enslavers, liars, perjurers, and whatever else is contrary to sound doctrine, in accordance with the gospel of the glory of the blessed God with which I have been entrusted. (1 Tim. 1:8–11)

Thus, when we use the law as a blunt instrument designed to reveal sin, we are safe. However, when we try to use it as a scalpel to circumcise the heart, we miss the mark.

A second temptation to an overreliance on moralism is the prevalence of sin. Of course, sin has *always* been prevalent. However, as we watch the news from day to day, we are bombarded with horrific examples of man's inhumanity to man. We see the picture of moral degradation described in Romans 1 in high definition clarity. And a love for the law of God coupled with the bombardment of the sinful culture around us often leads to moralistic responses. "We just need to put prayer back in schools." Or, "None of this would happen if Christians would just vote like the Bible tells them to."

Not only do we hear these types of responses all the time; we offer them ourselves. It is as though we grow weary of the gospel. It sounds too redundant to remind my children of their need for Christ; they just need to "stop doing that!" We don't have time to share the gospel with people around us. We do, however, have time to say, "That's wrong." It is much easier to snap back with another rule than it is to do heart surgery with the gospel. And again, the law is good! People *do* need to pray. My children do need to "stop that!" However, praying, avoiding sin, or doing "good" in itself is not the answer. "We have all become like one who is unclean, and all our righteous deeds are like a polluted garment" (Isa. 64:6).

PEOPLE WANT MORALISM

We all want black-and-white rules. We want someone to tell us, "This is right . . . that is wrong." It's clean. It's simple. It requires little or no self-examination. Consequently, the legalist that resides in every last one of us wants law! Thus, those of us who teach the Bible (and we have the same tendency) get a unique kind of response from people when we give them moralism. "That's good preachin', Pastor!" In my experience, this kind of response almost always follows a law/rule/morality-based statement. It's a sort of, "Attaboy. You sure told them" response. And frankly, it feels good!

We all have to guard against this tendency. We look at the world through a lens that is calibrated for legalism. We see something sinful or unjust, and we know immediately (1) that it is wrong, and (2) what ought to be done instead. This is not wrong, *per se*; it's just not enough. Sure, Joseph's brothers were wrong to be filled with such hatred toward him. That's a no-brainer. However, did we need the story of Joseph to show us that? Certainly there's another point to be made.

Ultimately, we lean toward moralism because it's easy. Moralism is, as noted earlier, the low-hanging fruit. It's the way we're all wired, and it takes very little effort or creativity to pull off. And it feels good to boot. We all feel better when we're taking the speck out of someone else's eye. Especially when it looks nothing like our plank. In other words, it's easy for me to preach hard against plotting to murder your brother and then throwing him in a pit to be sold into slavery when I've never done anything of the sort.

Several years ago, the Southern Baptist Convention passed a resolution against alcohol consumption. The resolution read:

> RESOLVED, That we urge that no one be elected to serve as a trustee or member of any entity or committee of the Southern Baptist Convention that is a user of alcoholic beverages.

Aside from the terrible wording of the resolution (i.e., this statement technically excludes anyone who eats chicken marsala), it has zero scriptural support.[3] However, it is incredibly easy to adopt such a resolution. The SBC has never had a problem with drunkenness among its clergy or denominational leaders. The SBC is by and large a teetotaling bunch. Hence, it took absolutely *no courage* to pass this statement.

On the other hand, the SBC considered another resolution the same year calling for integrity in church membership. That resolution did not pass. What would it have required? Simply that churches be honest about how many members they have and clean up their roles of inactive, nonexistent members that inflate their numbers. The drinking which nobody does (the speck) was much easier to deal with than the bearing false witness (the log) that characterizes the overwhelming majority of the churches in the Convention.

The SBC is not alone in this hypocrisy. You and I do the exact same thing every time we read the Bible! More importantly, we act out our hypocrisy in practical ways every day of our lives. We look for specks in our children, our coworkers, our teammates, and our friends. And our hypocrisy infects the way we read the Bible in general, and Old Testament narrative in particular.

A MORALISTIC READING OF JOSEPH

According to a moralistic reading, Genesis 37 is a lesson in jealousy and bad parenting. We see the consequences of favoritism on Jacob's part and bitterness on the part of Joseph's brothers. The moral of the story is (1) don't pick favorites among your children, and (2) don't be jealous of your brothers.

Chapter 38 is a classic case of hypocrisy and immorality on the part of Judah. And, while it doesn't seem to fit in the narrative, the moral point is clear: adulterers will be found out. However, the heroine in this story is also an adulteress, but that little messy detail is often overlooked since it interferes with the obvious moral point.[4]

This leads us to what are by far the most popular portions of the narrative. In chapter 39, Joseph shows himself faithful to both the Lord and to his master, Potiphar, when he causes Potiphar's house to prosper and later resists the advances of Potiphar's wife. In chapter 40 we see Joseph rise to prominence once again, this time in prison! The usual moral here, as in the previous chapter, has to do with faithfulness in difficult circumstances. Joseph becomes a shining example of the way believers ought to live when the going gets tough.

Chapter 41 is definitely the apex of Joseph's character arc. In this chapter we see the familiar interpretation of dreams, the fulfillment of a promise made by his fellow inmate, and the ultimate expression of the recurring theme of being placed over the affairs of his captors. Only this time the one who puts Joseph in charge is the most powerful man in the world! Joseph has remained faithful, and God has rewarded him.

This stands as an example to all those who have been maligned or mistreated by sinful men. Just hang in there like Joseph, and you will get your reward in the end. Moreover, if you look closely, you will find several leadership principles that defined Joseph's life and aided his ascension.

Chapters 42–44 offer us a glimpse at the proper response to new-found power and position. I read one sermon that outlined more than half a dozen kinds of "power" we see exhibited in the life of Joseph. There is positional, situational, psychological, spiritual, and several other kinds of power. Joseph is the picture of power in these chapters, and there is much to be learned from him here if we are going to exercise power effectively. We could go on, but I think you get the point.

WHAT'S WRONG WITH ALL OF THIS?

Everything we've observed about the Joseph narrative is true. And anyone teaching the story in a manner commensurate with the brief outline I've just given would be showing faithfulness to the text. Joseph was faithful. His brothers were sinful. He was rewarded with position, power, and prominence. All true! However, let me ask you a question. What separates that telling of the story from any other moral tale?

, where is the good news? We've been reminded again
\eed to be faithful. But where's the hope that we can?
posed to try harder so that God can reward us?

, ..o you notice the materialistic bent? Joseph was faithful to his father and he got sold into slavery. He was faithful to his master and he got sent to prison. He was faithful in the prison and he got promoted to second-in-command to Pharaoh, himself. There you have it: faithfulness = material wealth, success, notoriety, etc. How is that different from a Hindu, Muslim, Buddhist, or plain old secular, irreligious tale? How is it distinct from *Aesop's Fables*? Because it mentions God as the source of the success? Is that all? *There must be something more!*

Finding that something more involves changing the way we read the Bible. If we read the Bible like a book of principles and principals, we will find precisely that. However, if we remember a few interpretive keys, we will find much more.

Indicatives and Imperatives

One of the most important hermeneutical keys we can use in interpreting biblical texts is the distinction between indicatives and imperatives. Technically, these terms refer to the "mood" of verbs (i.e., the indicative mood and the imperative mood). The indicative mood points to what something is, while the imperative mood points to what something does.

For example, "Therefore, my beloved, as you have always obeyed, so now, not only as in my presence but much more in my absence, work out your own salvation with fear and trembling" (Phil. 2:12). This is a classic imperative. "Work out" is a command, an imperative for the reader. However, the very next verse is in the indicative mood: "for it is God who works in you, both to will and to work for his good pleasure" (v. 13). Here we are not told to "do" anything. We are merely told of the reality that makes it possible for us to do anything.

Sometimes we find entire books divided by this distinction. For example, the first three chapters of Ephesians are indicative, but the last three, introduced by a "therefore" clause, contain imperatives *based on the indicatives in the first half.* This distinction is important for a couple of reasons.

First, if we mistake indicatives for imperatives, we will attempt to work for that which we can never accomplish. An indicative tells us who we are because of what God has done. Pursuing that in and of ourselves is a form of works righteousness. For example, the indicative declaration "the wicked flee when no one pursues, but the righteous are bold as a lion" (Prov. 28:1) is not an invitation to work toward becoming bolder. It is an indicative statement about what God has done in the life of the righteous. Thus, we can no more make ourselves bold than we can make ourselves righteous!

Second, if we mistake imperatives for indicatives, we will leave undone that which we ought to do. Imperatives are commands. They are to be done. When we read, "You shall not steal" (Ex. 20:15), we are reading an imperative, a command. Of course, the indicatives are still essential, since they motivate, equip, and enable us to accomplish the imperatives. Remember, "None is righteous, no, not one; no one understands; no one seeks for God" (Rom. 3:10–11). So when we read imperatives that involve understanding, seeking, or being righteous, we know that there are indicatives that must be in place first.

So how does this apply to the Joseph narrative? Is the Joseph narrative riddled with indicatives and imperatives? If so, how do we differentiate between the two?

We tend to moralize narrative passages because they are inherently indicative in nature. A narrative is a story, and stories will not contain clear imperatives unless a narrator interjects them for his readers. Think about it: when you tell your children a bedtime story, the imperatives have to be interjected. You have to come to the end (in the case of a fable) and point out the moral of the story.

At other times, we look to the narrative itself for imperatives. There are a few traps here as well. Sometimes the imperatives in a narrative come from an immoral or ungodly character. Therefore, when the queen in *Alice in Wonderland* declares, "Off with her head!" we know that we are not reading a divine imperative, but a flawed human one.

At other times, the appropriateness of some imperatives might not be clear. For example, when Joseph tells his brothers, "Do not be distressed or angry with yourselves because you sold me here" (Gen. 45:5), is he giving a general imperative for all those who have committed heinous sin against another? Is this a moral principle for the moment, or for all time? If we don't have answers to these questions, how can we be sure we are reading the story the way God intends?

As we read the story of Joseph, we must guard ourselves against the tendency to read it as a fable. The Joseph story does not begin with, "Once upon a time." This is not a fable! If we can remember this, it will take us a long way. We will recognize that we have, in large part, imposed our familiar understanding of the nature of narrative on this narrative. And in some cases, this has brought us to conclusions that are inconsistent with the intent of the author.

How, then, do we interpret the deeper theological meaning behind the text? Is there some guide that can give us a clue? The answer is yes. God has given us the New Testament!

The Role of the New Testament in Interpreting the Old

The Bible is not some disjointed collection of unrelated tales; it is a unit. Therefore, reading and understanding the Bible requires familiarity with, commitment to, and comprehension of the whole. This, of course, is a lifetime pursuit. Nevertheless, there are things we can do now that will put us on sound footing.

First, New Testament authors have addressed the Joseph narrative and can help us put it in perspective. The clearest, safest, and most instructive path to understanding the Old Testament is to rely on New Testament authors who (1) were closer to the events than we are; (2) wrote under the inspiration of the Holy Spirit; (3) were direct disciples of the Son of God who used the Old Testament to teach them; (4) used the Old Testament extensively to communicate the gospel Christ gave them; and (5) were, in many cases, Jews who grew up with the Old Testament text.

All this means we need to look to the New Testament whenever possible to find our bearings in the Old Testament. In the case of the Joseph narrative, two main places (and two New Testament authors) deal with the story. Luke gives us a glimpse into the proper interpretation and proclamation of Joseph's life in his account of Stephen's sermon (Acts 7). The author of Hebrews gives us another example as he recounts Joseph's story in the "Faith Hall of Fame" in Hebrews 11. We will examine both.

Even when New Testament authors do not address the Joseph story directly, they address the moral, theological, and historical issues present in the narrative. New Testament authors deal with things like jealousy, bitterness, hatred, murder, forgiveness, and reconciliation. All these and more riddle the Joseph narrative from beginning to end. Thus, rather than wracking our brains to find what we "feel" or "think" Moses is trying to say, our primary inclination must be to interpret Old Testament texts in light of the way they are fleshed out in the New Testament.

Christ: The Interpretive Key to the Old Testament

A broader and more significant principle of interpreting the Old Testament is found in Christ. He is, in fact, the interpretive key to the Old Testament. This is not merely conjecture or opinion. Jesus teaches as much from his own mouth in a number of instances.

In one passage (that we usually fly right by), Jesus says to the Pharisees, "If you believed Moses, you would believe me; for [Moses] wrote of me" (John 5:46). Think about that for a minute. What did Moses write? He wrote the Pentateuch, the first five books of the Bible. Jesus says that the first five books of the Bible are about him. By the way, the first of those first five books is Genesis. Therefore, *Jesus taught that Genesis was about him.*

Jesus wasn't the only one to make note of this fact. After being called to follow Christ, "Philip found Nathanael and said to him, 'We have found him of whom Moses in the Law and also the prophets wrote, Jesus of Nazareth, the son of Joseph'" (John 1:45). Philip not only saw Christ in the Pentateuch, but also in the Prophets. This is confirmed in

Acts 8, when Philip confronts the Ethiopian eunuch as he reads from Isaiah: "And the eunuch said to Philip, 'About whom, I ask you, does the prophet say this, about himself or about someone else?' Then Philip opened his mouth, and beginning with this Scripture he told him the good news about Jesus" (vv. 34–35). Thus, Philip preached the gospel of Jesus Christ from Isaiah.

Nowhere is this idea that the Old Testament points to Christ communicated more clearly than in the Lord's discourse on the road to Emmaus:

> And he said to them, "O foolish ones, and slow of heart to believe all that the prophets have spoken! Was it not necessary that the Christ should suffer these things and enter into his glory?" And beginning with Moses and all the Prophets, he interpreted to them in all the Scriptures the things concerning himself. (Luke 24:25–27)

Jesus makes it clear that (1) the Old Testament spoke of him, and (2) it did so in a manner sufficiently clear as to call into question those who missed it. Moreover, having made these points, he begins right where we find ourselves, "with Moses," and goes on to demonstrate how the entire Old Testament points to himself.

WHAT THIS DOES AND DOES NOT MEAN

This does not mean that morality is irrelevant. One of the chief complaints against the redemptive-historical approach to Scripture is that it promotes antinomianism, or at least that it emphasizes indicatives at the expense of imperatives. In other words, redemptive-historical preaching is seen as "soft on sin" because it doesn't press people to action or obedience, but instead calls upon them to simply rest in Christ's redemptive work.

In fact, I was the object of a public protest after preaching a message on the life of Joseph at a prominent church in the Deep South. This particular church is known for high-octane moral preaching, which is one reason I chose my particular text that day. For the most part, the reception of the message was phenomenal. Christ's sheep really do hear his voice (John 10:27), and the people of God are hungry for the gospel, especially when they've been steeped in moralism. However, this can also create suspicion.

The lead instigator of the protest wrote me a long e-mail with an excerpt from a lecture about the dangers of redemptive-historical preaching. He accused me of, among other things, failing to celebrate Joseph's faithfulness in the face of trials, and, by extension, not calling God's people to persevere. Ironically, when I wrote him back with several concrete examples of where I had done precisely that, he told me that it was too late—the public protest, in the form of picketers outside the church, had already taken place.

This interaction highlighted both the principal concern of those unfamiliar with or suspicious of redemptive-historical preaching, and the sad reality that people's appetites have been so affected by moralism that when they hear something else, they assume it's not right.

This does not mean that we find Jesus in every verse. Another objection to the redemptive-historical approach to Old Testament narrative is that it inevitably leads to allegorizing the text. Suddenly, every part of the story refers to an aspect of Christ. The pit can't just be a pit; it has to be a type of grave. The prison can't just be a prison; it has to be a type of hell. And, of course, coming out of prison and going before Pharaoh must be a type of resurrection. The possibilities are endless, and the dangers, myriad.

However, as we will see, this is not at all what is being suggested here. Joseph's story must be read and understood in its immediate context before we can even begin to put it in its broader, redemptive-historical context. And while there are definitely types and shadows, the goal is not to find those everywhere, but to recognize them when the narrative makes them obvious.

This does *mean we read the story of Joseph in light of Christ.* Reading the Bible is challenging! Where do I start? How do I know what's going on? How much background do I need to know? These are just a few of the questions that paralyze many a Christian who knows he should read the Bible, but just can't quite get in gear. Now we're adding what appears to be another barrier between the believer and his or her ability to approach the Scriptures with confidence. However, that's not the case at all!

Far from making the Bible more difficult to read and understand, the approach we will take in this book is designed to make the Bible more accessible. We're taking what we already know—the story of God's redemption of sinners through the person and work of Christ—and using it as a grid through which we interpret all of Scripture. We're unlocking the Old Testament!

Granted, our task will still require some work. However, once we understand that the Old Testament is all about Christ and his redemptive work, much of the confusion over application is taken away.

IS THERE ANY GOOD NEWS?

"By faith Joseph, at the end of his life, made mention of the exodus of the Israelites and gave directions concerning his bones" (Heb. 11:22). That's it. That's how the author of Hebrews views the crux of the Joseph narrative. Not a word about all the things we make such a big deal of in our efforts to apply the text. For the author of Hebrews, Joseph's story is about faith—a faith that allowed him to look beyond Egypt to the exodus.

The good news in the story of Joseph is not that he went "from the pit to the palace." If it were, then the palace would be the end of the story. As it stands, the palace only gets us halfway. The palace is good news in the temporal sense, but no more. If we were merely a temporal people, that would be enough. But we are more than that. We were made for eternity. And unless there's something in the story of Joseph that gets us ready for, closer to, or more informed about that, there's no good news at all.

As God would have it, there *is* more to the story. There is good news. There is a message of redemption in the temporal as well as the eternal sense. There is a story of a people from whom will come a Savior, through whom will come redemption. That, my friend, is the good news. And the story of Joseph is full of it.

2

LAND, SEED, COVENANT

Part of the difficulty in tackling the story of Joseph is that it is found in what is arguably the most substantial book in the entire Bible. Genesis is not only a long book; it is also quite dense. Genesis lays the groundwork for our cosmology (doctrine of creation), our theology (doctrine of God), our anthropology (doctrine of man), our hamartiology (doctrine of sin), our soteriology (doctrine of salvation), our christology (doctrine of Christ), our pneumatology (doctrine of the Holy Spirit), and our eschatology (doctrine of last things). And that's just the first three chapters!

How, then, can we take the story of one character without examining the whole? How can we see the story of Joseph without seeing how it fits into the bigger picture of who man is, who God is, what sin is, what salvation is, and who Christ is? In short, we cannot understand Joseph until we understand Genesis. And that is the main reason we get Joseph so wrong.

Let's look, then, at this long, dense, historical, theological, philosophical gold mine called Genesis. We'll start by examining the structure and divisions of the book with a view toward placing Joseph's life and times in historical and theological context. In order to do that, we'll need to follow two major streams. First, we'll look at the obvious divisions Moses gave us directly, then we'll look at the not-so-obvious ones that he undoubtedly expected us to discern.

THE TOLEDOT

The first and most obvious way to divide Genesis is by taking note of the eleven mile markers Moses gives us, called *toledots*. *Toledot* is the Hebrew word for *generations, genealogy,* or *family line*. The English translation is, "These are the generations of." This phrase occurs eleven times in Genesis (Gen. 2:4; 5:1; 6:9; 10:1; 11:10, 27; 25:12, 19; 36:1, 9; 37:2), and serves to alert the reader to pivotal transitions. As Ray Dillard and Tremper Longman note in their introduction to the Old Testament, "The book of Genesis has a prologue (1:1–2:3) followed by ten episodes. The person named is not necessarily the main character but the beginning point of the section that also closes with his death."[1]

The Heavens and the Earth: The Toledot of Creation (Gen. 2:4)

The first toledot in Genesis is unusual because it references the generations not of a person, but of the heavens and the earth. We'll say more about this later. For now, it is important to note that Moses wastes no time in giving us these clues concerning the divisions of the book. Right after the creation account, he gives us a toledot, thus introducing perhaps the most important concept in Genesis.

Adam: The Toledot of the Fall (Gen. 5:1)

The next toledot begins a series of ten that all refer to the major (and a few minor) players in Genesis. This one, however, is perhaps the most important because it is the touchstone for all the rest. The promise of a Redeemer back in Genesis 3:15 serves as a catalyst for tracing the lineage of Adam to the one who will crush the head of the snake and restore what Adam has lost.

We must ask ourselves how Joseph's life connects to this toledot if we are to see him in the context of the entire book of Genesis. What does Joseph have to do with the promised seed? Is he in the line of the promised seed?[2]

Noah: The Toledot of De-creation (Gen. 6:9)

The next toledot takes us from the fall to the flood. Noah's generation is characterized by unmatched, unchecked, unquenchable desire and sin.

The LORD saw that the wickedness of man was great in the earth, and that every intention of the thoughts of his heart was only evil continually. And the LORD regretted that he had made man on the earth, and it grieved him to his heart. So the LORD said, "I will blot out man whom I have created from the face of the land, man and animals and creeping things and birds of the heavens, for I am sorry that I have made them." (Gen. 6:5–7)

Noah's generation is important for the unfolding of the rest of redemptive history. Jesus mentions Noah's day/generation in reference to his own second coming (Matt. 24:37–39; cf. Luke 17:26–28). Peter points to Noah as a picture of the coming judgment (2 Pet. 2:4–6).

Again, there is a clear link between this toledot and the story of Joseph. What is Joseph's story about if not the preservation of God's elect by his sovereign hand in the midst of catastrophe? Noah had his flood; Joseph had his famine.

Noah's Sons: The Toledot of Re-creation (Gen. 10:1)

The next two toledots introduce an important idea that runs throughout the book of Genesis. This toledot mentions three men as opposed to one. In the generations of Adam, the focus was on tracing the promised seed through the godly line of Seth. Here, we do not yet know which son will produce the promised seed, and we have record of all their generations.

Again, this figures into a proper understanding of the Joseph narrative (which we will explore later). Only one of Noah's three sons could be next in line. However, all of them were important to the development of the story.

Shem: The Toledot of God's New People (Gen. 11:10)

The toledot of Shem represents a return to the promised seed. His brothers were each important; however, only one can be the promised seed. Shem is the line through which the hope of God's elect continues.

Terah: The Toledot of Transition (Gen. 11:27)

Perhaps the oddest toledot is that of Terah. Terah did not perform great feats, exercise great faith, or commit great sins. There are just a few verses about Terah. However, his presence is pivotal. Terah is an important bridge to the next, and perhaps most central figure in Genesis, Abraham, who, by the way, has no toledot. He also connects Abraham to the de-created and the re-created world (which we will discuss further when we look at the land and the patriarchs), establishes the relationship between Abraham, Sarah, and Lot, and places Abraham in Ur of the Chaldeans.

Ishmael: The Toledot of Unbelief (Gen. 25:12)

Ishmael, like Esau after him, is an ironic toledot. Ishmael is a picture of unbelief and sin. He is not the promised seed. In fact, he represents Abraham and Sarah's attempt to "manufacture" the promised seed on their own. Instead of trusting the God who promised, they acted on their own, and suffered the consequences.

Ishmael does, however, become a people (Gen. 17:20). Three things about this fact are relevant to our discussion about the life of Joseph. First, Ishmael's mother was an Egyptian (25:12). Second, God told Abraham that Ishmael "shall be a wild donkey of a man, his hand against everyone and everyone's hand against him, and he shall dwell over against all his kinsmen" (16:12). Finally, when Joseph is sold into slavery in Egypt, it is a group of Midianite traders who purchase him (37:28). The Midianites are descendants of Ishmael. Clearly, this toledot bears upon our understanding of the life of Joseph.

Isaac: The Toledot of Promise (Gen. 25:19)

The toledot of Isaac reminds us of several things. First, his story reminds us of the providence of God as he accomplishes the impossible in order to bring his promise to pass. Second, Isaac's sin reminds us of the need for a redeemer. Isaac is, obviously, not the promised seed because of his character or faith, but in spite of his lack thereof. Finally, Isaac's marriage, and the lengths to which Abraham went to arrange it, lay the groundwork for the marriage of Jacob (which does not go well). This helps to put Joseph's life in perspective when we arrive at his marriage.

Esau: The Toledot of Election (Gen. 36:1, 9)

Esau's toledot is unique in that it is the only toledot repeated twice. Both mentions come in the same chapter, however, so there may be nothing to it. Regardless, the toledot of Esau completes a pattern. Three times—the toledot of Noah's sons, the toledot of Ishmael, and the toledot of Esau—Moses highlights the relationship between the promised seed and other offspring. Each time, the offspring that is not the offspring of promise is mentioned first.

The point here is clear: the promised seed is not a matter of circumstance, but one of election, sovereignty, and providence. Both Ishmael and Esau were firstborn, but neither was the promised seed. In Ishmael's case, one could argue that the problem was his parentage. But Esau and Jacob are twins. The message and the pattern are clear: God's electing grace does not depend on circumstance.

This pattern is played out in Joseph's life more than once. First, his firstborn brother, like Ishmael and Esau in previous generations, was not the promised seed. Second, when Joseph's sons are adopted by his father, Jacob, they are not blessed according to their birth order. Hence, again, we see that the story of Joseph cannot be understood properly apart from the broader context of the book of Genesis.

Jacob: The Toledot of a New Nation (Gen. 37:2)

The final toledot is that of Jacob. Jacob's story represents the culmination of all the previous historical and theological streams in Genesis. Jacob's birth reminds us that the promised seed has nothing to do with birth order. Jacob's marriage takes us back to when Abraham's servant found Isaac's wife. Jacob's name change reminds us of God's promise to establish a people. And Jacob's material acquisitions remind us of God's providential care for his people.

We must not miss the fact that this is the final toledot. This is important for a number of reasons, not the least of which is that it tells us that Joseph's story is actually part of Jacob's story. In other words, the toledot of Jacob forces us to look beyond Joseph to understand the meaning of Joseph's life.

LAND, SEED, COVENANT

Like changing seasons that mark the pattern of time, the themes of land, seed, and covenant appear again and again in the book of Genesis to mark the progression of redemptive history. And just as seasons are sometimes more or less pronounced, so these themes arrive on the scene sometimes with the fury of a heat wave or a blizzard, and other times with the subtlety of an autumn rain. Nevertheless, they are always there. And they are always reminding us of God's redemptive work.

Land

"In the beginning, God created the heavens and the earth" (Gen. 1:1). The Bible's opening words are among the most familiar and the most profound words ever written. With one line, Moses introduces God as the eternal, omnipotent, sovereign Creator of all things. He also introduces one of the three principal themes running through the entire book: the land. The land is the place where God's creative work takes place; it is the place where God makes and meets man; it is the substance out of which he makes man.

The land is also the source and location of the first toledot: "These are the generations of the heavens and the earth when they were created, in the day that the LORD God made the earth and the heavens" (Gen. 2:4).

The land is the stage where the story of redemptive history literally comes to life. Like man, however, the land suffers the effects and consequences of the fall (Gen. 3:17). But also like man, the land is subject to God's mercy, promise, and providential care. As God redeems man, he also redeems the land. Moreover, there is a special relationship between the men God redeems and the land he restores.

The Fall and the Land

The instant Adam fell into sin, his place in the land was jeopardized. He was no longer welcome in the land God had made for him to thrive:

Then the LORD God said, "Behold, the man has become like one of us in knowing good and evil. Now, lest he reach out his hand and take also of the tree of life and eat, and live forever—" therefore the LORD God sent him out from the garden of Eden to work the ground from which he was taken. He drove out the man, and at the east of the garden of Eden he placed the cherubim and a flaming sword that turned every way to guard the way to the tree of life. (Gen. 3:22–24)

Just like that, the perfect, pristine environment Adam knew was gone. From the point of eviction on, he would strive to re-create that which he had known, while the land would thwart him at every turn.

The theme of the land continues in the generations of Noah, both negatively and positively. Negatively, the land is seen as the locale of man's great sin:

When man began to multiply on the face of the land and daughters were born to them, the sons of God saw that the daughters of man were attractive. And they took as their wives any they chose. Then the LORD said, "My Spirit shall not abide in man forever, for he is flesh: his days shall be 120 years." (Gen. 6:1–3)

The idea of man's multiplying on the face of the land is a positive expression carried over from the dominion mandate in Genesis 1:28. However, as a direct result of the fall, even the multiplication is sinful. And not just sinful, but notoriously so:

The LORD saw that the wickedness of man was great in the earth, and that every intention of the thoughts of his heart was only evil continually. And the LORD regretted that he had made man on the earth, and it grieved him to his heart. So the LORD said, "I will blot out man whom I have created from the face of the land, man and animals and creeping things and birds of the heavens, for I am sorry that I have made them." But Noah found favor in the eyes of the LORD. (6:5–8)

Again, notice the references to the earth/land. The place God had made for human flourishing has become the place of his debasement. Now the land that was the place of creation in Genesis 1 becomes the place of de-creation in chapter 6:

> Now the earth was corrupt in God's sight, and the earth was filled with violence. And God saw the earth, and behold, it was corrupt, for all flesh had corrupted their way on the earth. And God said to Noah, "I have determined to make an end of all flesh, for the earth is filled with violence through them. Behold, I will destroy them with the earth." (6:11–13)

As God's patience runs out, there is a sense of inevitability that builds and demands resolution. Finally, God purges the land:

> The waters prevailed above the mountains, covering them fifteen cubits deep. And all flesh died that moved on the earth, birds, livestock, beasts, all swarming creatures that swarm on the earth, and all mankind. Everything on the dry land in whose nostrils was the breath of life died. He blotted out every living thing that was on the face of the ground, man and animals and creeping things and birds of the heavens. They were blotted out from the earth. (Gen. 7:20–23)

The land, thus having been purged, goes from a place of de-creation to one of re-creation. The story then moves from the generations of Noah and his sons to those of the patriarchs.

The Patriarchs and the Land

With Adam expelled from the garden and mankind destroyed and purged from the land, the narrative moves forward as God reiterates the mandate to be fruitful and multiply (Gen. 8:17; 9:1, 7) and ultimately calls a specific people to a specific land for a specific purpose (12:1–3). God begins by calling Abraham out of the land of Ur of the Chaldeans. However, the quest for the Land of Promise is not consummated until the very end—not the end of Genesis, but the end of redemptive history. In Genesis, we see only glimpses of fulfillment.

Abraham claims a portion of his inheritance when he purchases land in the Promised Land to bury Sarah:

> So the field of Ephron in Machpelah, which was to the east of Mamre, the field with the cave that was in it and all the trees that were in the field, throughout its whole area, was made over to Abraham as a possession in the presence of the Hittites, before all who went in at the gate of his city. After this, Abraham buried Sarah his wife in the cave of the field of

Machpelah east of Mamre (that is, Hebron) in the land of Canaan. The field and the cave that is in it were made over to Abraham as property for a burying place by the Hittites. (Gen. 23:17–20)

Eventually, Abraham joins his wife in her burial place (Gen. 25:7–11), and Isaac and Rebekah later join them, as does Jacob (Gen. 35:29; 49:31; 50:4–14). Thus, the patriarchs enjoy a sort of "already/not yet" relationship to the land promise. They are certainly in the land God promised, but their descendants are not. Moreover, it is not until the Promised Seed, Jesus, comes on the scene that we are able to understand that not even the land of Canaan is sufficient to express the greater reality of what God promised.

Joseph and the Land

What, then, does the theme of the land have to do with the life of Joseph? This question must be answered if we intend to interpret the story of Joseph rightly. It is significant that Joseph's story starts in Canaan, the Land of Promise, but ends in Egypt, the land of suffering and oppression. As we come to the Joseph narrative, this contrast will prove quite significant.

Seed

While the land is the place where the drama of redemptive history plays out, the seed is the mechanism by which redemption is accomplished. Thus, there is an important relationship between the land and the seed.

Creation and the Seed

As we noted earlier, the creation account starts with the land. God creates the heavens and the earth, and then separates waters from land. While the waters contain a significant portion of God's creation, the land is the setting for his crowning glory of creation: man. However, the narrative moves quickly from the land to the seed. The means by which everything in the earth multiplies (including man) is the seed:

And God said, "Let the earth sprout vegetation, plants yielding seed, and fruit trees bearing fruit in which is their seed, each according to its kind, on the earth." And it was so. The earth brought forth vegetation, plants yielding seed according to their own kinds, and trees bearing fruit in which is their seed, each according to its kind. And God saw that it was good. And there was evening and there was morning, the third day. (Gen. 1:11–13)

The command to "be fruitful and multiply and fill the earth and subdue it" (Gen. 1:28) assumes the role of the seed in multiplication. The very next verse reiterates this principle: "And God said, "Behold, I have given you every plant yielding seed that is on the face of all the earth, and every tree with seed in its fruit" (v. 29). However, the real significance of the seed comes into play two chapters later, when the interaction between man and fruit leads to the most important statement about "seed" in the entire Bible.

The Fall and the Seed

When Eve, tempted by the Serpent, eats the fruit from the tree of the knowledge of good and evil and gives the fruit to Adam, the entire biblical narrative changes forever. God curses the Serpent and promises that his demise (and man's redemption) will come about through a process that relies on the principle of multiplication and seed: "I will put enmity between you and the woman, and between your offspring [seed] and her offspring [seed]; he shall bruise your head, and you shall bruise his heel" (Gen. 3:15).

This promise sets in motion a conflict that will ebb and flow from the next chapter of Genesis through the end of redemptive history.

In Genesis 2, the seed of the Serpent, Cain, kills the seed of the woman, Abel (Gen. 4:8; cf. 1 John 3:12). Then in Exodus, the Serpent comes after the male seed again: "Then the king of Egypt said to the Hebrew midwives, one of whom was named Shiphrah and the other Puah, 'When you serve as midwife to the Hebrew women and see them on the birthstool, if it is a son, you shall kill him, but if it is a daughter, she shall live'" (Ex. 1:15–16).

This scene is repeated in the opening book of the New Testament as the Promised Seed, Jesus, comes into the world:

> Then Herod, when he saw that he had been tricked by the wise men, became furious, and he sent and killed all the male children in Bethlehem and in all that region who were two years old or under, according to the time that he had ascertained from the wise men. (Matt. 2:16)

And, as if providing a bookend at the close of God's account of redemptive history, the book of Revelation captures the essence of this timeless battle:

> And another sign appeared in heaven: behold, a great red dragon, with seven heads and ten horns, and on his heads seven diadems. His tail swept down a third of the stars of heaven and cast them to the earth. And the dragon stood before the woman who was about to give birth, so that when she bore her child he might devour it. (Rev. 12:3–4)

Thus, the principle of the fall and the seed is also the message of redemption. This Promised Seed is not the product of the fall; he is the answer to it. It is because of the Promised Seed that we have hope. As we trace the Promised Seed's line throughout Genesis, we see the first glimpses of that hope as God restores the line through Seth, preserves it through the flood in Noah and his sons, and then expands it to a nation through the patriarchs.

The Patriarchs and the Seed

Much has already been said about tracing the line of the Promised Seed through the patriarchs. It is important here, though, to remember that this process is inexorably linked both to what came before and what comes after. It is impossible to understand the significance of the patriarchal line apart from understanding the promise of Genesis 3:15. Moreover, it is equally futile to understand the significance of this line apart from the arc of redemptive history.

The patriarchs are more than mere examples. In fact, they are, by and large, pretty poor examples. They are significant because they are tangible evidence of God's faithfulness to his promise. Neither infertility, in the case of Abraham and Sarah, nor deception, in the case of Jacob and Leah, can thwart God's plan to bring about the redemption of his people through the promised seed.

Joseph and the Seed

What, then, does the theme of the seed have to do with the life of Joseph? Joseph is not the promised seed. The question we must ask, then, is, what is the significance of Joseph's relationship to the promised seed? Again, to ignore this question is to fail to understand Joseph in the context of Genesis as a whole and in the context of specific themes and divisions of Genesis into which he is placed.

Covenant

The third theme running throughout the Genesis narrative, without which it is impossible to interpret the story properly, is the theme of covenant. From the covenant of works, which Adam broke, to the Noahic covenant after the flood, to the Abrahamic covenant, Genesis is a book of covenants. In fact, the word *covenant* appears more than twenty-five times in Genesis.

Creation and Covenant

The first covenant we encounter in Genesis is the covenant God makes with Adam. This covenant, often referred to as the "covenant of works," is introduced in Genesis 2:

> The LORD God took the man and put him in the garden of Eden to work it and keep it. And the LORD God commanded the man, saying, "You may surely eat of every tree of the garden, but of the tree of the knowledge of good and evil you shall not eat, for in the day that you eat of it you shall surely die." (vv. 15–17)

Adam was created perfect, innocent, and capable of keeping this covenant. However, he did not. As a result, he and all his posterity fell into sin. This brought a curse on the land, and now toil, strife, and physical death are the normal, unavoidable experience of all mankind (3:17–19).

The Fall and Covenant

Both the theme of covenant and the consequences of Adam's failure to keep the first one are carried forward in Genesis, and beyond. We see the horrible consequences of sin just a few chapters later during the life of Noah, when "the Lord saw that the wickedness of man was great in the earth, and that every intention of the thoughts of his heart was only evil continually" (6:5). We saw earlier, in reference to the land, that this resulted in a purging.

However, in relation to the theme of covenant, there is hope in spite of judgment. The Noahic covenant resulted in the most famous covenant sign of all: the rainbow.

> Then God said to Noah and to his sons with him, "Behold, I establish my covenant with you and your offspring after you, and with every living creature that is with you, the birds, the livestock, and every beast of the earth with you, as many as came out of the ark; it is for every beast of the earth. I establish my covenant with you, that never again shall all flesh be cut off by the waters of the flood, and never again shall there be a flood to destroy the earth." And God said, "This is the sign of the covenant that I make between me and you and every living creature that is with you, for all future generations: I have set my bow in the cloud, and it shall be a sign of the covenant between me and the earth. When I bring clouds over the earth and the bow is seen in the clouds, I will remember my covenant that is between me and you and every living creature of all flesh. And the waters shall never again become a flood to destroy all flesh. When the bow is in the clouds, I will see it and remember the everlasting covenant between God and every living creature of all flesh that is on the earth." God said to Noah, "This is the sign of the covenant that I have established between me and all flesh that is on the earth." (Gen. 9:8–17)

Note that six of the twenty-six uses of the word *covenant* occur in this single passage! Thus, the most infamous, awesome, and terrible expression of God's wrath against man in the entire Bible is followed by one of the most explicit promises/covenants in Scripture. How dare we attempt to understand Genesis, or the life of Joseph, without taking this into account?

The Patriarchs and Covenant

The most famous covenant in Genesis is found in chapter 12. Ironically, the word *covenant* is nowhere to be found in the text. Nevertheless, the covenant itself is clear:

> Now the LORD said to Abram, "Go from your country and your kindred and your father's house to the land that I will show you. And I will make of you a great nation, and I will bless you and make your name great, so that you will be a blessing. I will bless those who bless you, and him who dishonors you I will curse, and in you all the families of the earth shall be blessed." (vv. 1–3)

Notice the presence of all three key elements in this single passage. God sends Abram to go to a *land*, promises to bless him with *seed* (offspring), and does so by way of *covenant*. This, again, is key to interpreting Genesis. As we come to the life of Joseph, we cannot forget that his significance is tied up in the Abrahamic covenant.

Joseph and Covenant

Obviously, we must ask ourselves how the Joseph narrative figures into the concept of covenant that runs so deeply throughout the book of Genesis. If we understand the themes of seed, land, and covenant, we will see Joseph's story through an entirely different light than perhaps we're used to. More importantly, viewing Joseph through this threefold lens doesn't just give us a different perspective; it gives us the perspective that God, through Moses, intended us to have.

CONCLUSION

Neither land, seed, nor covenant finds its consummation in the book of Genesis. Genesis ends with God's covenant people not only out of the land, but in Egypt, the opposite of the Land of Promise. The promised seed is traced to Judah, but the blessing given to him in Genesis 49 makes it clear that the ultimate Promised Seed is still yet to come. Finally, the covenant cannot be consummated without the land and the seed. Therefore, we must look beyond Genesis (and certainly beyond Joseph) if we are to understand God's plan of redemption.

3

JUXTAPOSITION

GENESIS 37–38

Joseph is one of three major biblical characters in whom no sin is revealed. Like Jesus and Daniel, Joseph is presented as a flawless hero. However, while Jesus is in fact sinless, the same is not true of Joseph and Daniel. Thus, we must be careful not to assume that the absence of information about Joseph's sinfulness is meant to indicate anything about his need for a Savior.

Like a diamond against black felt, the character of Joseph shines against the backdrop of his brothers' sin. This is not a reflection on Joseph. He, like all of Adam's descendants, is a sinner (Rom. 3:1–10). The temptation is to view Joseph as an example of sinless perfection. However, that is not the author's intent. Moses is not trying to paint a portrait of Joseph; he is displaying God's glory. In order to do this, he juxtaposes the best of Joseph with the worst of his brothers.

THE FAVORITE SON (GEN. 37:2–11)

These are the generations of Jacob.

Joseph, being seventeen years old, was pasturing the flock with his brothers. He was a boy with the sons of Bilhah and Zilpah, his father's wives. And Joseph brought a bad report of them to their father. Now Israel loved Joseph more than any other of his sons, because he was the son of his old age. And he made him a robe of many colors. But when his brothers saw that their father loved him more than all his brothers, they hated him and could not speak peacefully to him. (Gen. 37:2–4)

The toledot of Jacob turns immediately into the story of Joseph. This, along with the fact that Jacob is either a minor player or completely absent from this section of the narrative, can lead the reader to assume that this section is not about Jacob at all. However, that would be a mistake. The pattern of the book of Genesis, along with the ultimate resolution of the narrative, makes it clear that this is indeed all about Jacob, the last of the patriarchs. But Jacob's story cannot be told without this focus on Joseph.

God is indeed going to make Jacob/Israel a great nation, and Joseph will be the primary means by which that task is accomplished. Jacob has neither the character nor the wisdom to become that which God intends. Nevertheless, God will raise him up in spite of himself. Jacob picks Joseph as his favorite son despite having seen the damage that favoritism caused in his own family. Ironically, it is this sinful favoring of Joseph over the other sons that sets in motion a series of events that will result in Jacob losing his favorite son for the majority of his remaining days.

A Bad Report

The first piece of evidence of Moses's real intent is the almost immediate introduction of a bad report. We get a brief introduction of Joseph in the form of his name, age (seventeen), parentage (not from one of the concubines), occupation (shepherd), and the fact that he brought a bad report against his brothers. In this context, the bad report serves to present Joseph's brothers as the "bad guys" in the narrative. They are immediately presented as the sinful actors whose deeds will require God's intervention on Joseph's behalf. This story, like the rest of the Bible, is all about sin and redemption.

At this point, many readers tend to fill in the blanks in the narrative. Joseph is often colored as a tattletale who earned his brothers' hatred by repeatedly bringing bad reports in an effort to get them in trouble. However, this assumption goes beyond the narrative. There is not a negative word about Joseph in the entire story. The author doesn't say anything about tattling. We do, however, get a glimpse into Joseph's role in the family when Jacob sends him on a fact-finding mission and asks him to bring word back (37:14).

A Bad Parent

While Joseph is innocent in the matter, Jacob is not. Jacob continues the tradition of bad parenting practiced by his father, Isaac. This is evident in Jacob's actions in 37:3: "Now Israel loved Joseph *more than any other of his sons*, because he was the son of his old age. And he made him a robe of many colors." Just as Isaac had chosen Esau over Jacob, Jacob now chooses Joseph over his brothers. At this point, the careful reader must wonder why Jacob would subject his children to the same treatment that had so ravaged his life as a young man. But Moses leaves no doubt as to which side of the ledger Jacob belongs. He, like his sons, is a sinful actor whose deeds will require God's intervention. He, too, is a sinner in need of a Savior.

A Bad Feeling

The first verses of Genesis 37 establish the tension between Joseph and his brothers, a tension that explains their unthinkable actions. His brothers "hated him and could not speak peacefully to him" (v. 4). Here there is a double juxtaposition. First, there is the juxtaposition of obedient and disobedient sons. Second, there is the juxtaposition of Jacob's love for Joseph and his brothers' hatred for him. This is not an exaggeration. We learn later in the narrative that Joseph's brothers actually contemplated killing him before deciding, at Judah's prompting, to sell him into slavery. This is the dark piece of felt against which the brilliance of Joseph's obedience will shine as the narrative moves along.

THE OBEDIENT SON (GEN. 37:12–17)

It is not enough to know that Joseph's brothers (and his father) were flawed, sinful men. Moses intends for us to see the distinction be-tween Joseph and his brothers. He does this first through a simple yet profound episode wherein Joseph does nothing more than obey the will of his father:

> Now his brothers went to pasture their father's flock near Shechem. And Israel said to Joseph, "Are not your brothers pasturing the flock at Shechem? Come, I will send you to them." And he said to him, "Here I am." So he said to him, "Go now, see if it is well with your brothers and with the flock, and bring me word." So he sent him from the Valley of Hebron, and he came to Shechem. And a man found him wandering in the fields. And the man asked him, "What are you seeking?" "I am seeking my brothers," he said. "Tell me, please, where they are pasturing the flock." And the man said, "They have gone away, for I heard them say, 'Let us go to Dothan.'" So Joseph went after his brothers and found them at Dothan. (Gen. 37:12–17)

The brilliance of Joseph's character is seen in the magnitude of the task with which he is entrusted, his instant, unwavering commitment to obey, and the persistence with which he pursues completion of the task.

The Magnitude of the Task

As a boy, one of my least favorite tasks was to go to the store for my mother. It wasn't that I didn't love my mother; it was just, well, far! From our apartment to the store was a little over a mile. Not a country mile, mind you. This was a city mile. This was South Central Los Angeles in the late 1970s to early 1980s. I couldn't ride my bike for fear that it would be stolen. Thus, I had to walk more than a mile . . . both ways . . . uphill . . . in the snow! And I was no older than ten. Still, this journey paled in comparison to the journey on which Joseph embarked in Genesis 37.

Anyone who has ever had a seventeen-year-old son can imagine what it would be like to send him on a multiday, fifty-mile journey alone, on foot or beast of burden. The modern mind boggles at the very thought. Will he be safe? Will he get lost? Will he be afraid? Will his food and water last? And, in Joseph's case, will he come to harm when he encounters his brothers? This was a monumental task. As such, it serves to highlight Joseph's obedience.

The Instant, Unwavering Commitment to Obey

Joseph's only words in the passage are, "Here I am." There is not a hint of hesitation or wavering. This is the epitome of obedience. The phrase "here I am" occurs eight times in Genesis: three times in reference to the sons of the patriarchs responding to their fathers (22:7; 27:1; 37:13), one time in reference to the patriarch responding to his son (22:18), and four times in reference to the patriarchs responding to God himself (22:1, 11; 31:11; 46:2). If Joseph had any fears or doubts, they were not recorded in the text. The point here is clear: Joseph is an obedient son.

The Persistence to Complete His Task

The only thing more impressive than the magnitude of the task and Joseph's instant, unwavering commitment to obey is the persistence with which he pursued his assignment. Upon arriving at the place he was told to go, Joseph discovered that his brothers had gone several miles farther seeking good pastureland. Instead of checking the task off his list and returning home with a less-than-complete report, Joseph went even farther in an effort to acquire the information his father was seeking.

THE SINFUL SONS (GEN. 37:18–36)

In stark contrast to Joseph's obedience, Moses presents the rest of Jacob's sons as a unified band of hate-filled, murderous, disobedient men whose hearts are set on anything *but* their father's desires. Remember, rightly or wrongly, Joseph *was* their father's favorite son, and they knew it.

> They saw him from afar, and before he came near to them they conspired against him to kill him. They said to one another, "Here comes this dreamer. Come now, let us kill him and throw him into one of the pits. Then we will say that a fierce animal has devoured him, and we will see what will become of his dreams." But when Reuben heard it, he rescued him out of their hands, saying, "Let us not take his life." And Reuben said to them, "Shed no blood; throw him into this pit here in the wilderness, but do not lay a hand on him"—that he might rescue him out of their hand to restore him to his father. So when Joseph came to his brothers, they stripped him of his robe, the robe of many colors that he wore. And they took him and threw him into a pit. The pit was empty; there was no water in it. (Gen. 37:18–24)

JOSEPH AND THE GOSPEL OF MANY COLORS

This is far more than a "be like the good son, not like the bad sons" story. This juxtaposition serves to highlight Joseph's obedience and add tension to the narrative. That tension grows in the next scene:

> Then they sat down to eat. And looking up they saw a caravan of Ish-maelites coming from Gilead, with their camels bearing gum, balm, and myrrh, on their way to carry it down to Egypt. Then Judah said to his brothers, "What profit is it if we kill our brother and conceal his blood? Come, let us sell him to the Ishmaelites, and let not our hand be upon him, for he is our brother, our own flesh." And his brothers listened to him. Then Midianite traders passed by. And they drew Joseph up and lifted him out of the pit, and sold him to the Ishmaelites for twenty shekels of silver. They took Joseph to Egypt. (Gen. 37:25–28)

Several important factors are worth noting here. First, the intro-duction of the Ishmaelites harkens back to an earlier part of the Gen-esis narrative. Ishmael was the illegitimate son of Abraham who not only was rejected as the promised heir, but about whom an ominous prophesy was given: "He shall be a wild donkey of a man, his hand against everyone and everyone's hand against him, and he shall dwell over against all his kinsmen" (Gen. 16:12).

Thus, in addition to the juxtaposition of an obedient son over against disobedient ones, there is also the juxtaposition of Ishmael's offspring and the offspring of his brother Isaac. The promised seed (Jacob) has come into the Promised Land in fulfillment of the cov-enant God made with Abraham. However, before the promised heir is revealed, the favorite son of the patriarch Jacob leaves the Promised Land, and is sold not only into slavery but into the hands of the descen-dants of Abraham's rejected heir.

The Other Land

The final paragraph of chapter 37 not only wraps up the initial conflict between Joseph and his brothers, but also introduces the juxtaposition that will dominate the rest of the Joseph story:

> When Reuben returned to the pit and saw that Joseph was not in the pit, he tore his clothes and returned to his brothers and said, "The boy is gone,

50

and I, where shall I go?" Then they took Joseph's robe and slaughtered a goat and dipped the robe in the blood. And they sent the robe of many colors and brought it to their father and said, "This we have found; please identify whether it is your son's robe or not." And he identified it and said, "It is my son's robe. A fierce animal has devoured him. Joseph is without doubt torn to pieces." Then Jacob tore his garments and put sackcloth on his loins and mourned for his son many days. All his sons and all his daughters rose up to comfort him, but he refused to be comforted and said, "No, I shall go down to Sheol to my son, mourning." Thus his father wept for him. Meanwhile the Midianites had sold him in Egypt to Potiphar, an officer of Pharaoh, the captain of the guard. (Gen. 37:29–36)

Reuben's plan to regain his father's favor is thwarted. The beloved coat of many colors is destroyed. The father who picked favorites has had his favorite taken away, and the central character in the narrative has moved progressively farther away from the Land of Promise, finally ending up not just in another country, but in Egypt, the land that will come to represent oppression and bondage throughout the rest of redemptive history.

TAKEAWAYS OF GENESIS 37

Genesis 37 is filled with lessons about the nature and consequences of jealousy, bitterness, anger, and more. However, there are far better places in the Bible from which to teach those things. For example, Genesis 37 serves as a tremendous illustration for James 4, but not the other way around. Narrative is, by definition, indicative. And the narrator of Genesis 37 does not stop to point out "truths to live by" as he tells this particular story. Moreover, this narrative is written in such a way that it presents facts, pieces of a puzzle. The main point is not that Jacob picked favorites, or that Joseph's brothers had murder in their hearts. There are truths that run much deeper. More importantly, there are truths that point us away from ourselves to a God who saves in spite of us.

Obedience Does Not Guarantee Success or Ease

One inescapable truth we find in Genesis 37 and elsewhere in the Joseph story is that obedience does not guarantee success or ease. The juxtaposition of Joseph's obedience and his brothers' disobedience is not the backdrop for a lesson about getting what you want (as we will see in Genesis 41). In fact, we see here and elsewhere that Joseph's obedience is rewarded with hardship. He ends up in a pit, then in Egypt, far away from the land and people of promise.

Ultimately, as Joseph leaves home to find his brothers, he moves farther and farther away from the Land of Promise. But here's something most readers never consider. When Joseph leaves home on this simple fact-finding mission, he leaves for the last time. *Joseph will never return to live in the land until his bones are brought back after the Exodus* (Ex. 13:19). In fact, it is this aspect of Joseph's story that warranted mention in the "Faith Hall of Fame" (Heb. 11:22). This is not a feel-good story wherein the hero returns victorious. This is a tale of redemption in which Joseph pays an unthinkable price for a purpose much greater than he.

This is an important truth for God's people to understand. In fact, one of my greatest problems with the typical *Aesop's Fables* approach to the Joseph narrative is the tendency to reduce his story to a "hang in there, you'll be rewarded in the end" tale. The truth is, God's people suffer! "Indeed, all who desire to live a godly life in Christ Jesus will be persecuted" (2 Tim. 3:12). The lives of some faithful Christians end in martyrdom. If we fail to read Joseph's story properly, we will have absolutely no understanding of that reality.

God's Electing Work Is Not Based on Man's Performance

Joseph may be the star of the show, but he is *not* the promised seed. Just as his father Jacob was chosen in spite of the fact that Esau was his father's favorite, so Joseph would have to give way to Judah. In both cases, the choice of the promised seeds had absolutely nothing to do with anything they had done. We know this because the Bible makes it clear that the choice of Jacob over Esau happened "though they were not yet born and had done nothing either good or bad—in order that God's purpose of election might continue, not because of works but because of him who calls" (Rom. 9:11). This was true for Jacob, Judah, and every other human being upon whom God's favor has fallen.

Sin Makes Us Blind to Our Greatest and Only Hope

To be sure, Joseph's brothers are first-class sinners. Not only are they murderers (see Genesis 34), they are also filled with jealousy, which is identified as one of the vilest of sins: "Let us walk properly as in the daytime, not in orgies and drunkenness, not in sexual immorality and sensuality, not in quarreling and jealousy" (Rom. 13:13). However, their greatest problem is that their sin blinds them to their greatest and only hope.

Joseph has dreams that point to his ultimate role as the savior of the family. He foresees his elevation to prominence in Egypt, and, by extension, his part in delivering his family from famine. However, all his brothers (and his father) can see is that Joseph's dreams point to his superiority, something that Jacob has conditioned them to resent. As a result, when they see the young man whom God has designated to save their lives walking toward them in obedience to his father, their first inclination is to kill him.

Interesting, isn't it? Joseph is not presented as a "type" of Christ. However, his brothers' response to him mirrors the response of sinners to Jesus in the New Testament. Jesus comes as "the Lamb of God, who takes away the sin of the world!" (John 1:29), and the ultimate response is, "Crucify him" (Mark 15:13–14; Luke 23:21; John 19:6, 15; see Matt. 27:31; Mark 15:20). But in Jesus's case, there was no Judah to calm the crowd and change their minds.

JOSEPH AND JUDAH: THE FAVORITE SON VS. THE PROMISED ONE (GENESIS 38)

Perhaps the most confusing aspect of the story of Joseph is the seemingly out-of-place excursus into Judah's "wanderings" in Canaan. It is confusing because of the abrupt change from the intriguing, fast-paced narrative of the life of Joseph. The story leaves him as a slave in Egypt with no resolution to his dilemma, and jumps to Judah marrying and having children with a Canaanite woman:

> It happened at that time that Judah went down from his brothers and turned aside to a certain Adullamite, whose name was Hirah. There

> Judah saw the daughter of a certain Canaanite whose name was Shua. He took her and went in to her, and she conceived and bore a son, and he called his name Er. She conceived again and bore a son, and she called his name Onan. Yet again she bore a son, and she called his name Shelah. Judah was in Chezib when she bore him. (Gen. 38:1–5)

The significance of Judah's marriage is threefold. First, we have already seen how important the marriages of their children are to the patriarchs. Abraham made his servant swear that he would "not take a wife for [his] son from the daughters of the Canaanites" (Gen. 24:3). Now we find Judah, the next in the line of the Promised Seed, doing precisely that. This raises questions about the *seed*.

Second, not only does Judah end up with a Canaanite, but he "went down from his brothers and turned aside." This raises questions about the *land*. Judah wasn't sold into slavery. Nor was he advancing the patriarch's acquisition of territory. No one forced him to abandon the Land of Promise; he simply departed on his own. This is an amazing juxtaposition.

Third, the narrative makes it clear that Judah has not just left for a short while. He is among the Canaanites long enough for the woman to conceive three times. Even if she was exceptionally fertile, this took at least two-and-a-half to three years. How could Judah have been raised by the last of the patriarchs, tasted the Land of Promise, and decided to "turn aside" to live among the Canaanites? This raises questions about *the covenant*. Is Judah part of the covenant people of God? Of course, this question will be answered later. Nevertheless, the point is clear: Moses is showing how far Judah has fallen.

Disobedience and Death

Genesis 38 is also filled with a dark sort of irony. Judah has participated in deceiving his father by making him think that the son whom he loved was killed. Now, within the span of a few verses we see that God has killed two of Judah's three sons:

> And Judah took a wife for Er his firstborn, and her name was Tamar. But Er, Judah's firstborn, *was wicked in the sight of the* Lord, *and the* Lord

put him to death. Then Judah said to Onan, "Go in to your brother's wife and perform the duty of a brother-in-law to her, and raise up offspring for your brother." But Onan knew that the offspring would not be his. So whenever he went in to his brother's wife he would waste the semen on the ground, so as not to give offspring to his brother. And *what he did was wicked in the sight of the* LORD, *and he put him to death also.* Then Judah said to Tamar his daughter-in-law, "Remain a widow in your father's house, till Shelah my son grows up"—for he feared that he would die, like his brothers. So Tamar went and remained in her father's house. (Gen. 38:6–11)

As we have seen with Abraham, Isaac, and Jacob, there can be no promised seed apart from God's providential intervention. Judah's case is no different. He is a wicked man with wicked sons. He has married outside of the godly line, and he is quickly losing heirs at the hand of God himself, due to their wickedness. Eventually, Judah's wife will also die.

TAKEAWAYS OF GENESIS 38

The application of Genesis 38 can be baffling. The series of negative lessons and warnings are obvious. The idea of sexual purity is low-hanging fruit. However, as in the case of Genesis 37, there are much clearer teachings in the Bible on this topic. Also like Genesis 37, this narrative is more indicative than imperative, lending itself much more effectively to the role of illustration. Nevertheless, the passage has several redemptive-historical implications.

The Land Apart from the Promise Is a Curse Instead of a Blessing

Ironically, as Judah ran away from his brothers, he ran farther into the land that was promised to his forefather, Abraham. However, unlike earlier scenes where the patriarchs incrementally acquired more and more of the land, symbolizing their future possession of the promise, this narrative foreshadows a much harder truth: being in the Land of Promise can be a curse as well as a blessing.

The land has no magical qualities that will make God's people happy, content, successful, or better. There is not a physical place on

JOSEPH AND THE GOSPEL OF MANY COLORS

earth that can do that. A disobedient member of the covenant community will find folly and judgment wherever his feet may trod. Thus, Judah can find himself in the place God promised without the peace God promised.

Ultimately, the land is merely a shadow of things to come. Israel will go in and out of the land throughout her history. The only time there will be true peace and conquest is in the New Jerusalem (Rev. 3:12; 21:2).

Election Does Not Equal Ease and Earthly Success

Judah is the heir of promise, the forefather of Jesus Christ! Nevertheless, he has lost two sons at the hand of God due to their wickedness and disobedience. Moreover, after Judah's wife dies, his daughter-in-law uses his own indiscretion to deceive him into fathering her children (Gen. 37:12–30). This is anything but a picture of earthly success! Granted, Judah's life will change eventually. For now, though, he is the epitome of salvation by grace alone.

The People of God Have Always Been Multiethnic

Despite her deception, Tamar bears not only twins, but an heir of promise. Her name is forever written in the genealogy of the Promised Seed, Jesus Christ (Matt. 1:3). This is significant for a number of reasons, not least of which is that she is a Gentile.

God promised Abraham that he would be the father of many nations and that in him all the nations of the world would be blessed (Gen. 12:1–3). The addition of Tamar in the royal line is part of the fulfillment of this promise. Of course, the grafting in of the Gentiles (Romans 11) through faith in Christ is the greater manifestation of this reality. Consider Romans 9:

> But it is not as though the word of God has failed. For not all who are descended from Israel belong to Israel, and not all are children of Abraham because they are his offspring, but "Through Isaac shall your offspring be named." This means that it is not the children of the flesh who

qZzX9

are the children of God, but the children of the promise are counted as offspring. (vv. 6–8)

Ultimately, the story of Judah and Tamar is an encouragement to all who sin and are in need of a Savior, whether Jew or Greek, slave or free, male or female (Gal. 3:28). Judah reminds us that salvation is of the Lord. Tamar reminds us that salvation is "to the Jew first and also to the [non-Jew]" (Rom. 1:16). They both remind us that God was at work bringing about our redemption by preserving a family line that would eventuate in the Promised Seed, Jesus Christ.

LOOKING AHEAD

As we turn from chapter 38 to the rest of Joseph's story, we must remember that Joseph's story is not essentially about Joseph. God is doing much more than just preserving, sustaining, and promoting the patriarch's favorite son. The insertion of the story of Judah and Tamar reminds us of that. Of course, if we do not take the long view, chapter 38 makes no sense. In fact, it may cause us to agree with textual critics who see its existence as cause for doubting the inerrancy of Scripture.

But when we view chapter 38, and the rest of the narrative, through the lenses of seed, land, and covenant, a more accurate picture begins to take shape. Now let us turn our attention back to the journey of the principal character in this portion of the narrative, Joseph. We will find that things have gone from bad to worse for the dreamer.

4

PROVIDENCE

GENESIS 39-40

Genesis 39 has a clear theme. Four times we read that the Lord was with Joseph (vv. 2, 3, 21, 23). One need not wonder what the author is trying to communicate here. This is not a lesson about fleeing sexual temptation (though the passage does provide the most vivid picture of such); this is a lesson in divine providence.

Most Christians use the word *providence* as a substitute for *luck*. If we swerve our car and miss oncoming traffic, we say, "That was providential." If the doctor finds our cancer early enough to treat it successfully, again we say, "That was providential." However, this is *not* the doctrine of divine providence. The providence of God doesn't just cover the near miss; it also covers the fatal crash and the terminal diagnosis.

Understanding the doctrine of providence is the key to interpreting the life of Joseph rightly. If we do not understand providence, we will not understand the significance of the events before us in these chapters. Moreover, a failure to comprehend the providence of God has led to perhaps the greatest misunderstanding of all in the life of Joseph: the interpretation of his ascension to power in chapter 41 as the culmination of God's providential work in his life.

DIVINE PROVIDENCE: MORE THAN CHRISTIAN "LUCK"

Seeing God's providence in the life of Joseph is about more than looking for the "good" outcome. We're able to understand this when we have a proper definition of providence. While *sovereignty* addresses God's authority to rule and govern his creation, *providence* addresses the manner in which he does so. Wayne Grudem's definition is about the clearest and most accessible I've found, and it will serve our purpose well:

> We may define God's providence as follows: God is continually involved with all created things in such a way that he (1) keeps them existing and maintaining the properties with which he created them; (2) cooperates with created things in every action, directing their distinctive properties to cause them to act as they do; and (3) directs them to fulfill his purposes.[1]

God Keeps Things Existing and Maintains Their Properties

The first key to understanding God's providence is to understand the manner in which he relates to his creatures. Why am I not a man today and a fish tomorrow? Why does the sun continue to rise in the east and set in the west? The answer is providence. When we speak of God's providence we mean, as Charles Hodge has noted, "that all things out of God owe the continuance of their existence, with all their properties and powers, to the will of God."[2] Everything is what it is and acts as it does by God's providence.

This means that God did not have to make Joseph's brothers feel toward him as they did, or change the nature of the Midianite traders or the Egyptian captain in order for Joseph to end up in Egypt. He did, however, orchestrate these things in accordance with the properties with which he had created each actor.

God Cooperates with Created Things to
Cause Them to Act as They Do

God is more than just a divine watchmaker. He does more than just endow his creation with certain properties and watch it go. As the Baptist theologian John Gill noted, God "looks down upon the earth, takes notice and care of all his creatures in it, and makes provision for them, and guides and directs them to answer the ends for which they were made." The key word there is "guides." There is a delicate balance between guidance toward God's ends, and man's pursuit of his own.

Imagine that you are presented with three types of ice cream: vanilla, chocolate, and strawberry. Are you free to choose? Before you answer, consider this: You did not choose your taste buds. You did not choose your first experience with each of these flavors. You didn't even choose the circumstances that ultimately provided you with these three choices. All of these things (your particular properties and the properties of the other actors) came about providentially. Thus, as you make your "choice," we can say with confidence that it is not without God's providence.

The same can be said of the actors who have conspired to bring Joseph to this point. God "cooperated" with Joseph's brothers, the Midianite traders, and the Egyptian captain of the guard as they acted in accordance with, not in opposition to, their independent, God-given properties.

God Directs All Things to Fulfill His Purpose

Having created all things with specific properties and cooperating with those properties, God causes those things to fulfill his purpose. This is the crucial point. Providence does not mean (as the "Christian luck" theory implies) that God orchestrates only things that we find pleasurable, profitable, or preferable to us, but that he orchestrates *all* things in a manner befitting his redemptive purposes. Therefore, as the Second London Baptist Confession rightly states, "There is not any thing, befalls any by chance, or without his Providence" (5.2).

This may sound like theological hairsplitting; however, it is crucial to understanding God's providence in general, and the exercise of his providence in the life of Joseph. Again, if providence is no more than Christian luck, Genesis 39 is void of providence, and the repeated phrase "God was with Joseph" is confusing at best. However, if we understand providence rightly, we read Genesis 39 with renewed interest and insight.

THE PROVIDENTIAL JOURNEY FROM POTIPHAR TO PRISON (GENESIS 39)

His master saw that the LORD was with him and that the LORD caused all that he did to succeed in his hands. So Joseph found favor in his sight and attended him, and he made him overseer of his house and put him in charge of all that he had. From the time that he made him overseer in his house and over all that he had, the LORD blessed the Egyptian's house for Joseph's sake; the blessing of the LORD was on all that he had, in house and field. So he left all that he had in Joseph's charge, and because of him he had no concern about anything but the food he ate. (Gen. 39:3–6)

The story line couldn't be more intentional. Four times in four verses Moses reminds us of God's hand in Joseph's circumstances: "His master saw that the LORD was with him" (v. 3a); "the LORD caused all that he did to succeed in his hands" (v. 3b); "the LORD blessed the Egyptian's house for Joseph's sake" (v. 5a); and "the blessing of the LORD was on all that he had, in house and field" (v. 5b). But note that providence here is mixed with irony.

When we were introduced to Joseph, he was looking after his father's house; here he is in service to an Egyptian captain. Earlier in the narrative, God was prospering Jacob, multiplying his wealth by showing favor in his shepherding of the sheep. Now, an Egyptian is becoming prosperous because of the Lord's hand in the life of the son of the patriarch. Nevertheless, the Lord is at work governing Joseph's every step.

Providential Purity

Most people who have heard a sermon on Genesis 39 have probably heard it from the perspective of Joseph's commitment to sexual purity. Of course, there are several points to be made about that. For instance, Joseph's encounter with Potiphar's wife is a clear contrast to Judah's encounter with Tamar in chapter 38. However, from a practical standpoint, several aspects of the story don't quite fit the average man's experience with sexual temptation:

Now Joseph was handsome in form and appearance. And after a time his master's wife cast her eyes on Joseph and said, "Lie with me." But he refused and said to his master's wife, "Behold, because of me my master has no concern about anything in the house, and he has put everything that he has in my charge. He is not greater in this house than I am, nor has he kept back anything from me except you, because you are his wife. How then can I do this great wickedness and sin against God?" And as she spoke to Joseph day after day, he would not listen to her, to lie beside her or to be with her. (Gen. 39:6–10)

Here again we see God's providence as Joseph maintains faith in the God of his forefathers in spite of his circumstances. However, his reward is not what one would expect, especially if we were operating from the conventional view of providence. We would expect Joseph's faithfulness to be rewarded with deliverance. Perhaps Potiphar would discover his wife's treachery, or God would have him reassigned to a better post. But that is not the case. God, in his providence, had other plans.

The Providence of Betrayal

But one day, when he went into the house to do his work and none of the men of the house was there in the house, she caught him by his garment, saying, "Lie with me." But he left his garment in her hand and fled and got out of the house. And as soon as she saw that he had left his garment in her hand and had fled out of the house, she called to the men of her household and said to them, "See, he has brought among us a Hebrew to laugh at us. He came in to me to lie with me, and I cried out with a loud voice. And as soon as he heard that I lifted up my voice and cried out, he left his garment beside me and fled and got out of the house." Then she laid up his garment by her until his master came home, and she told him the same story, saying, "The Hebrew servant, whom you have brought among us, came in to me to laugh at me. But as soon as I lifted up my voice and cried, he left his garment beside me and fled out of the house." (Gen. 39:11–18)

There it is: Joseph's reward for faithfulness and purity. Betrayal. This is the part that fits awkwardly into that sermon about holding fast and fleeing temptation. Instead of happily ever after, this story goes from frying pan to fire.

The Providence of Prison

I've met men who've told me that the best thing that ever happened to them was going to prison. In fact, I've been told this very thing on more than one occasion while preaching in prison. In each instance the men shared tales of out-of-control sin, addiction, violence, and worse. Their lives were spinning out of control, and the only way out was death—or so they thought. Then they went to prison and met God! I never tire of hearing such stories of brands plucked from the fire.

However, Joseph's life wasn't falling apart. He wasn't on a fast track to death and destruction. Joseph did not need to be "rescued" from his circumstances. Nevertheless, prison was exactly where he needed to be in order to fulfill God's plan. And while he would not know that for quite some time (more than a decade, in fact), God's providence was still governing his steps:

> As soon as his master heard the words that his wife spoke to him, "This is the way your servant treated me," his anger was kindled. And Joseph's master took him and put him into the prison, the place where the king's prisoners were confined, and he was there in prison. But the LORD was with Joseph and showed him steadfast love and gave him favor in the sight of the keeper of the prison. And the keeper of the prison put Joseph in charge of all the prisoners who were in the prison. Whatever was done there, he was the one who did it. The keeper of the prison paid no attention to anything that was in Joseph's charge, because the LORD was with him. And whatever he did, the LORD made it succeed. (Gen. 39:19–23)

Again, the narrative leaves no room to doubt God's providence. Just as Genesis 39 began with repeated assurances of the Lord's presence with Joseph, here at the end it mentions God's providence three times: "the LORD was with Joseph and showed him steadfast love and gave him favor in the sight of the keeper of the prison" (v. 21); "the LORD was with him" (v. 23b); "whatever he did, the LORD made it succeed" (v. 23c). Again the providence of God is evident despite what appears to be disastrous. But these are just the obvious references to God's providence; there are others.

First, "imprisonment was not a standard punishment for crimes."[3] Potiphar could easily have had Joseph executed, but he did not. Second, Joseph was not sent to just any prison; he ended up in the place where the king's prisoners were confined. This is a foreshadowing of the next phase in Joseph's providential journey, Pharaoh's court. In fact, the king (or Pharaoh) is mentioned nine times in chapters 39 and 40 (Gen. 39:1; 40:1–2, 5, 13–14, 17, 19), like breadcrumbs leading us toward chapter 41.

TAKEAWAYS OF GENESIS 39

As noted earlier, the low-hanging fruit in Genesis 39 is Joseph's sexual purity. However, most men who struggle with sexual sin don't have to worry about their master's wife finding them so irresistible that she beckons them continually until she finally rips their clothes off. Of course, for those who do, this is the perfect text! For the rest of us, there are passages like Matthew 5:27–30 that offer much more pertinent instruction. The author of Genesis has much more in mind. Certainly we should "flee from sexual immorality" (1 Cor. 6:18). But that's not the main point here.

God Is Present with His People Even in the Worst Circumstances

The most comforting words in this chapter are, "God was with Joseph." That phrase is the key to understanding Genesis 39. The message here is not "resist sexual temptation so that you, too, can end up in prison." The message here is the providence of God! God is with his people. Joseph finds himself in slavery, away from the Land of Promise—far from his father's house, but not beyond the Lord's reach.

As a pastor, I've had to walk with people during some of the most difficult circumstances imaginable. During those times, it is incredibly comforting to know that we serve a God who is there! "My son was falsely accused, and is on his way to prison. Where is God?" He's in the same place he was when Joseph was falsely accused and sent to prison. Which, by the way, is the same place he was when his only begotten

Son was falsely accused and sentenced to death! This will not turn our mourning into laughter, but it will most assuredly redirect our focus and remind us of our only source of hope.

Obedience to God Does Not Guarantee Favor with Men

Here's where we leave the American dream behind. We've all heard the stories of people like Abraham Lincoln, Bill Gates, Oprah Winfrey, Michael Jordan, and others, who prove that all you need is a little ingenuity, hard work, and a break here and there, and you, too, can go from nothing to something . . . *big*! We tell our children all the time that hard work and integrity will pay off in the end, that the Lord will reward their faithfulness. And I'm not saying that we shouldn't say those things. God has given us an entire book in the Bible, the book of Proverbs, dedicated to these types of expressions of wisdom.

However, Joseph's experience is as real as Lincoln's or Jordan's. Obedience sometimes results in more hardship. Sometimes telling the truth gets you fired. Sometimes playing by the rules gets you a fourth-place ribbon while cheaters win gold, silver, and bronze. And sometimes, refusing to go along with the wishes of an adulteress gets you thrown in prison.

Our hope, however, is in God's ultimate justice and his providence. "We know that for those who love God all things work together for good, for those who are called according to his purpose" (Rom. 8:28). The key here is God's *purpose*. We cannot separate providence from purpose, or substitute our purpose for his. This is as true for us as it was for Joseph, as we shall soon see.

No Matter How Bad Things Are, They Can Still Get Worse

This sounds like a very discouraging statement. However, allow me to explain before passing judgment. Sharon is a young professional who postponed motherhood to pursue a career. Eventually, she came to realize that time was running out and that she was not trusting God with the circumstances of her life. Convinced that the time had come to stop postponing parenthood, she and her husband decided to get pregnant.

Several years later, after having experienced a number of miscarriages, Sharon finally carried a baby to term. The miscarriages had taken a toll on her in a number of ways; she had never known such loss and despair. However, she and her husband had clung to their faith, and now their perseverance had resulted in a beautiful baby girl.

Weeks later, Sharon's husband died suddenly and unexpectedly. Instantly, Sharon went from being a happy new mother with a long-awaited baby to being a young widow and a single mom. She was devastated. Why would God do this? Certainly she had experienced more than her share of loss with the multiple miscarriages. Why would God answer her prayer for a baby only to take her husband? What had she done to deserve this?

I don't pretend to know the answer to these questions. However, I do know that God's providence is about his purposes, not ours. "The secret things belong to the LORD our God" (Deut. 29:29). I know that God was willing to crush and kill his spotless, sinless Son for his own glory and for the salvation of his elect. How, then, can I fault him when flawed, sinful men, who deserve death and hell, endure hardship and frowning providences on their way to inheriting salvation and glory?

Joseph's journey from Potiphar to prison is a reminder that God does not balance the scales in the here-and-now. He certainly doesn't always tilt them in our individual favor. He does, however, work all things according to the counsel of his perfect, immutable will, and he uses frowning providences to accomplish his redeeming work. Therein lies our hope. Thus, we can say with Job, "Though he slay me, I will hope in him" (Job 13:15).

PROVIDENCE AND INTERVENTION (GENESIS 40)

Chapter 40 is a chapter of transition. The prison is merely a way station between the home of Potiphar, the captain of Pharaoh's guard, and the court of Pharaoh himself. We have already been told that this prison is "the place where the king's prisoners were confined" (39:20). Now we are introduced immediately to two such prisoners:

> Some time after this, the cupbearer of the king of Egypt and his baker committed an offense against their lord the king of Egypt. And Pharaoh was angry with his two officers, the chief cupbearer and the chief baker, and he put them in custody in the house of the captain of the guard, in the prison where Joseph was confined. The captain of the guard appointed Joseph to be with them, and he attended them. They continued for some time in custody. (Gen. 40:1–4)

Joseph has now gone from the captain of Pharaoh's guard, to the keeper of his prison, to his baker and his cupbearer. At each point he has, in God's providence, moved closer to the ultimate encounter for which he was sent to Egypt. Notice also that Joseph is now working "in the house of the captain of the guard, in the prison." Since Potiphar is referred to as the "captain of the guard" in 39:1, "it appears that Joseph is detained under Potiphar's supervision and is there again given authority."[4]

A Second Pair of Dreams

The word *dream* occurs nineteen times in the book of Genesis; all but five of them occur in the life of Joseph, between chapters 37 and 41. Two more occur in the story of Jacob, his father. Jacob's dream aided him as Laban plotted to take advantage of him, thus allowing Jacob to amass wealth (31:10). God came to Laban in a dream in order to protect Jacob from Laban's anger (v. 24).

The next pair of dreams occurs at the beginning of the "Joseph" portion of the narrative (37:5–6, 9–10). Then later, in the midst of Joseph's ordeal in Egypt, the theme of dreams and interpretation—something that has always signaled God's intervention on behalf of his family—suddenly appears again:

> And one night they both dreamed—the cupbearer and the baker of the king of Egypt, who were confined in the prison—each his own dream, and each dream with its own interpretation. When Joseph came to them in the morning, he saw that they were troubled. So he asked Pharaoh's officers who were with him in custody in his master's house, "Why are your faces downcast today?" They said to him, "We have had dreams, and there is no one to interpret them." And Joseph said to them, "Do

not interpretations belong to God? Please tell them to me." (Gen. 40:5–8)

In chapter 39 we are told that "God was with Joseph." In chapter 40, we actually see it. The God of Jacob is sending dreams to orchestrate events in the life of Jacob's favorite son. Joseph is not abandoned!

Forgotten . . . Again

On the third day, which was Pharaoh's birthday, he made a feast for all his servants and lifted up the head of the chief cupbearer and the head of the chief baker among his servants. He restored the chief cupbearer to his position, and he placed the cup in Pharaoh's hand. But he hanged the chief baker, as Joseph had interpreted to them. Yet the chief cupbearer did not remember Joseph, but forgot him. (Gen. 40:20–23)

That last statement is like a kick in the stomach. Just when it looks like Joseph's deliverance has come, the cupbearer forgets him. Later we will discover that this is merely a matter of timing; in the next verse we learn that, "After two whole years, Pharaoh dreamed . . ." (Gen. 41:1). But for now, this is just another discouraging moment in a series of discouraging moments that would cause anyone to despair. How do we find hope in this? How do we find encouragement?

TAKEAWAYS OF GENESIS 40

Genesis 40 is yet another chapter that, taken by itself, has very little "Christian" application. Is it all about dreams and interpretation? How about principles for advancement in the workplace? In either case, we can find material on that from multiple sources. The question is, how does this fit in God's plan of redemption? What does this teach those whose lives are "hidden with Christ in God" (Col. 3:3)?

The Circumstances of Our Service Do Not Determine the Value Thereof

I will never forget the first time I tried out for a football team. I was in junior high school. And like most of the guys on the field that day, I didn't have much experience. I was just a red-blooded American male trying to play America's game—football! As the coach divided the field into sections, a funny, yet predictable thing happened. The section for receivers, running backs, and quarterbacks was full. The section for linemen was virtually unoccupied. Everybody wanted the ball; nobody wanted to block.

Eventually reality set in, and not only were the ranks of skill players thinned out, some people were left wishing they had what it took to "at least" be a lineman! When it was all said and done, a few guys hung on to become water boys and team managers. In other words, we had a team. And every guy, regardless of his position, was an important part of that team—all the way down to the guy who held the coach's clipboard.

We went on to be city champs that year. When it was all said and done, even the water boys and team managers were proud to be associated with the team.

In some ways, that rather insignificant experience of mine mirrors a much more significant reality: "For just as the body is one and has many members, and all the members of the body, though many, are one body, so it is with Christ" (1 Cor. 12:12). And for Paul, there was no doubt that some of those members were slaves (1 Cor. 12:13; Gal. 3:28) and prisoners (Eph. 6:20).

In other words, serving God in the context of slavery or prison does not negate the fact that we are serving God! Moreover, when we understand the bigger picture of God's redemptive purpose, we know that he uses even our slavery, imprisonment, and everything else to bring about his desired ends:

> For consider your calling, brothers: not many of you were wise according to worldly standards, not many were powerful, not many were of noble birth. But God chose what is foolish in the world to shame the wise; God chose what is weak in the world to shame the strong; God chose what is low and despised in the world, even things that are not, to bring to nothing things that are, so that no human being might boast in the presence of God. And because of him you are in Christ Jesus, who became to us wisdom from God, righteousness and sanctification and

redemption, so that, as it is written, "Let the one who boasts, boast in the Lord." (1 Cor. 1:26–31)

God Is Actively Involved in the Affairs of His People Wherever They Are

It is important to remember that God is not the God of "big" things; he is the God of *all* things. Joseph had left the Land of Promise, but he had not left the realm of God's governance. As the psalmist sang:

> Where shall I go from your Spirit?
>   Or where shall I flee from your presence?
> If I ascend to heaven, you are there!
>   If I make my bed in Sheol, you are there!
> If I take the wings of the morning
>   and dwell in the uttermost parts of the sea,
> even there your hand shall lead me,
>   and your right hand shall hold me. (Ps. 139:7–10)

At times it seems as though our circumstances are too small or too unpleasant for God to be involved. Certainly he has bigger, more important things to attend to and more worthy servants in need of his care.

We mustn't forget that even the hairs on our heads are all numbered (Matt. 10:30; cf. Luke 12:7). There are no insignificant people in the redemptive plan of God. Not one of us is here by accident. And not one of our circumstances has taken God by surprise.

LOOKING AHEAD

Genesis 40 stands as a reminder that God is at work even when we cannot see or know what he is doing. When Joseph was on his way to visit his brothers, God had the pit in mind. When he was in the pit, God had Potiphar in mind. When he was with Potiphar, God had prison in mind, and when he was in prison, God had Pharaoh in mind. Eventually, we will see that even when Joseph is with Pharaoh, God has more than that in mind.

Believe it or not, Joseph's stint in prison has more to do with you and your salvation than you know. It is a mistake to take Joseph's current set of circumstances in isolation, not only because it limits our view of the greater narrative, but also because the greater narrative is the story of redemption.

It will be important to keep this in mind as we approach chapter 41. If we do not, we will fall into the all-too-familiar trap of treating the next chapter as if it were the last, when, in fact it is merely another stop on the journey to redemption. As we turn the page, we will examine what I believe is one of, if not the most, misunderstood and misinterpreted scenes in the entire Bible.

5

EXALTATION

GENESIS 41

Genesis 41 is the most pivotal chapter in the Joseph narrative. In fact, it is one of the most pivotal chapters in the entire Bible. It is also one of the most misinterpreted chapters in the Bible. Listen to ten messages on Genesis 41, and all ten will deal with what I call the "American Cinema" interpretation. We are so used to the character arc of modern movies that we read the Scriptures as if it were a screenplay. As a result, Genesis 41 *appears* to fit perfectly into a typical feel-good, after-school special.

In viewing Joseph's life this way, chapter 41 appears to be the big payoff we've been waiting for. He has remained faithful, and God is rewarding him with fame, fortune, and family. This is the moment when we look into the eyes of onlooking Sunday school children and say, "Boys and girls, remember this the next time people mistreat you." But is that correct? Does that interpretation fit the context of the narrative to this point? I think not.

Let's examine this part of the story the same way we've examined everything else up to this point, keeping in mind the major themes of *seed, land,* and *covenant*. But first, let me tell you a story. (It's a story most pastors have heard before.)

Helen is a concerned mother. She has a son named Christian who keeps her on her knees. She has frequently called upon the elders of her church to pray for her boy. Christian was always a talented, handsome young man. He went to a great university, earned an impressive degree, and landed a great job. Whatever he touched seemed to turn to gold. However, his pursuits came with a price.

Christian ended up working for a company whose moral reputation was less than desirable. He also moved quite far away from home—to another country, in fact. He never went to church, and he never saw his family, not even for holidays. Eventually, he even started to go by a different name. Nobody knew him as Christian; his friends called him Darwin because of his ability to thrive in their "survival of the fittest" company culture.

Eventually, Christian married an unbeliever, the granddaughter of one of the founders of the company. They had a couple of kids, but Helen never got to see them—she had never even seen a picture of her grandsons. She did know, however, that they had never seen the inside of a church. Needless to say, Helen was heartbroken!

Now, think about the elements of Helen's story. Did you notice where they came from? Apart from the obvious differences (i.e., Christian wasn't sold into slavery and forced into his situation), the rest of the elements come straight from Genesis 41! How on earth, then, can this chapter be considered the big payoff? Why do we hear Hollywood theme music when we picture Joseph standing next to Pharaoh? And why do we tell our children that this is what their faithfulness will bring? No, my friend, I think we've got it all wrong. I think we need to look at the key elements of this chapter again.

JOSEPH IS REMEMBERED

Genesis 41 opens with another series of dreams wherein Pharaoh sees fat, healthy cows being eaten by skinny, sick ones (vv. 1–4), and plump, healthy ears of grain being devoured by skinny, sick ones (vv. 5–7). "So in the morning his spirit was troubled, and he sent and called for all the magicians of Egypt and all its wise men. Pharaoh told them his dreams, but there was none who could interpret them to Pharaoh" (v. 8).

The flow of the narrative is unmistakable. This is the third pair of dreams in Joseph's life. He has been established as an interpreter of dreams, and Pharaoh needs one. Pharaoh has been mentioned numerous times in the narrative, each of Joseph's moves has brought him one step closer to the king, and now, the king needs exactly what Joseph has. And there's a man in Pharaoh's employ who knows it!

> Then the chief cupbearer said to Pharaoh, "I remember my offenses today. When Pharaoh was angry with his servants and put me and the chief baker in custody in the house of the captain of the guard, we dreamed on the same night, he and I, each having a dream with its own interpretation. A young Hebrew was there with us, a servant of the captain of the guard. When we told him, he interpreted our dreams to us, giving an interpretation to each man according to his dream. And as he interpreted to us, so it came about. I was restored to my office, and the baker was hanged." (Gen. 41:9–13)

Joseph is no longer forgotten! The cupbearer has remembered him at last. The result of all this? Joseph interprets Pharaoh's dreams and earns his release from prison.

THEN AND NOW: CONTRASTS IN JOSEPH'S LIFE

Interestingly, Moses has provided us with a clear path to understanding the nature of Joseph's dilemma. At every point, we see a direct contrast between where Joseph started and where he has ended up. These contrasts point us to a rather clear conclusion: Genesis 41 is *not* Joseph's payoff.

Pagan King/Kingdom vs. the Patriarch's House

The first contrast is between Pharaoh and Jacob. Joseph started his journey as the favorite son of the patriarch Jacob. He was looking after his father's affairs and was an asset in his father's house. Since then, he has been an asset to the captain of the guard and the keeper of the prison. Now he will serve a new master:

> This proposal pleased Pharaoh and all his servants. And Pharaoh said to his servants, "Can we find a man like this, in whom is the Spirit of God?" Then Pharaoh said to Joseph, "Since God has shown you all this, there is

none so discerning and wise as you are. You shall be over my house, and all my people shall order themselves as you command. Only as regards the throne will I be greater than you." (Gen. 41:37–40)

The irony is that Joseph is still a slave. More importantly, his master is a pagan who is worshiped as a god. The phrases Pharaoh uses are almost identical to those used in reference to Joseph's position in Potiphar's house in chapter 39: "From the time that he made him overseer in his house and over all that he had. . . . he left all that he had in Joseph's charge" (vv. 5–6). And when Joseph responds to the advances of Potiphar's wife, he says, concerning his master, "He has put everything that he has in my charge. He is not greater in this house than I am, nor has he kept back anything from me except you, because you are his wife" (vv. 8–9). In other words, Joseph is as much a slave in chapter 41 as he was two chapters earlier. However, since his new master is the most powerful man in the world, we tend to read the story differently.

Pagan Wealth vs. the Patriarch's Gift

We see the second contrast when Pharaoh places jewels and clothes on Joseph, just as his father had done:

> And Pharaoh said to Joseph, "See, I have set you over all the land of Egypt." Then Pharaoh took his signet ring from his hand and put it on Joseph's hand, and clothed him in garments of fine linen and put a gold chain about his neck. (Gen. 41:41–42)

Earlier we read, "Now Israel loved Joseph more than any other of his sons, because he was the son of his old age. And he made him a robe of many colors" (Gen. 37:3). One wonders if Joseph thought about the day his father gave him his special coat—and, perhaps, the day his brothers stripped him of it. In any case, the contrast is unmistakable.

Signet rings were used for signing official documents. Hot wax was poured, and the ring pressed against it to affix the king's official seal. Thus, giving Joseph the ring meant that Pharaoh was trusting him with his affairs, just as Jacob had done when Joseph was in his house. The linen robe is a more direct contrast, but the picture is clear: Joseph is in the wrong land serving the wrong leader of the wrong nation (Gen. 12:1–3).

Pagan Worship vs. the Patriarch's Adoration

The third contrast harkens back to the first pair of dreams recorded in the Joseph story. Remember, Joseph told his brothers, "And behold, your sheaves gathered around it and bowed down to my sheaf" (Gen. 37:7). Then, after his second dream, he included his father, at which point Israel responds, "Shall I and your mother and your brothers indeed come to bow ourselves to the ground before you?" (v. 10). Now, in the house of Pharaoh, we find a different story:

> And he made him ride in his second chariot. And they called out before him, "Bow the knee!" Thus he set him over all the land of Egypt. More-over, Pharaoh said to Joseph, "I am Pharaoh, and without your consent no one shall lift up hand or foot in all the land of Egypt." (Gen. 41:43–44)

Ironically, when Jacob heard Joseph's interpretation of his own dream, he didn't believe him. He and his sons were offended at the idea of bowing the knee before Joseph. Pharaoh has no such reservations. He sees Joseph's dreams as a word from on high sent to save him and his people. Jacob would have done well to respond likewise.

Pagan Identity vs. the Patriarch's Name

When we read, "And Pharaoh called Joseph's name Zaphenath-paneah" (Gen. 41:45), our minds ought to be drawn back to the other instances in the Genesis narrative where we've seen name changes, most signifi-cantly Abraham, who was first Abram; Sarah, who was first Sarai; and Israel, who was first Jacob.

In each instance, it was God who gave the name change. More-over, in the case of the patriarchs, the changes reflected covenantal significance. Abram was told, "No longer shall your name be called Abram, but your name shall be Abraham, for I have made you the father of a multitude of nations" (Gen. 17:5). When Jacob fought with the angel, he was told, "Your name shall no longer be called

Jacob, but Israel, for you have striven with God and with men, and have prevailed" (Gen. 32:28).

Joseph's name change, however, goes in the opposite direction. Joseph's name originally reflected Rachel's plea for God to give her another son (Gen. 30:24). While we have no idea what Zaphenath-paneah means, it most assuredly does not have the same significance, and probably has something to do with pagan deity. Whatever the name means, the significance of the name change is clear. Just as with Daniel, Hananiah, Mishael, and Azariah (Dan. 1:6–7), this name change has to do with masking, and/or altering Hebrew identity.

Why do we read the Babylonian name changes that occur in the book of Daniel negatively, but we do not view Joseph's Egyptian name change as being equally devastating? Certainly Daniel and his friends did not look back at Joseph's name change and say, "It was a good thing when it happened to him . . . perhaps it will be good for us." If we take off our Hollywood lenses, this is about as clear a sign as we will ever see in Scripture. Genesis 41 is *not* the big payoff.

Pagan Wife vs. the Patriarch's Provision

In Genesis 41 we discover that Pharaoh "gave [Joseph] in marriage Asenath, the daughter of Potiphera priest of On. So Joseph went out over the land of Egypt" (Gen. 41:45). This fifth contrast takes us all the way back to Genesis 24, when Abraham made his servant swear not to take a wife for his son from among the Canaanites, and Genesis 28:1–3, where Isaac repeats the same to Jacob.

Hence, just as Judah did in chapter 38, Joseph has broken with patriarchal tradition in marrying the Egyptian woman. Looking back at Abraham also reminds us that Hagar, too, was an Egyptian—just one more bread crumb leading us to a proper interpretation of this portion of the narrative.

At every point in the narrative, Moses points us in a singular direction. He reminds us again and again that this is not where Joseph belongs. Moses leaves absolutely no room for the notion that this is the big payoff. There is not a hint of Hollywood theme music. Neverthe-

less, we have continued to insist on interpreting this pa
tive otherwise. We convince ourselves that this portion (
exists to give us hope, when, in fact, it exists to give u
comes later.

IDENTIFICATION WITH THE PEOPLE AND LAND OF THE COVENANT

The first glimmer of hope comes when God blesses Joseph with children:

> Before the year of famine came, two sons were born to Joseph. Asenath, the daughter of Potiphera priest of On, bore them to him. Joseph called the name of the firstborn Manasseh. "For," he said, "God has made me forget all my hardship and all my father's house." The name of the second he called Ephraim, "For God has made me fruitful in the land of my affliction." (Gen. 41:50–52)

Here Joseph has a chance to reveal a bit of his character. Up to this point, other than Joseph's interpretation of Pharaoh's dreams, all we have seen are the actions of Pharaoh. Moses has not provided any insight into Joseph's reaction to all that has happened to him. Now we hear from the patriarch's favorite son. And his actions are clear, decisive, and in complete contrast to the typical interpretation of previous events.

Joseph identifies with the people of the covenant by giving his sons Hebrew names. As a slave, he had no choice but to receive the name (and the wife) Pharaoh gave him. However, when his own sons are born, he has a choice. Had he accepted his Egyptian identity—and more importantly, had he rejected his Hebrew identity—he would have given his sons Egyptian names. But he does not. This clearly reveals his loyalty to his father.

Consider for a moment the monumental significance of this simple gesture. I went to high school in San Antonio, Texas, with many a Jorge, Enrique, and Miguel, who went by George, Henry, or Mike when away from their homes. These young people had parents who were struggling to hold on to their Mexican identity and pass it on to their children. But for some of the students, this was too much to bear. They didn't want to spend their days with gringos butchering their names.

And some didn't want to be identified with a country, culture, and language that was as foreign to them as it was to the rest of their American peers. But their parents' goal of retaining their family culture was clear. Joseph, it seems, has the same goal.

Joseph's master is Egyptian. Joseph's wife is Egyptian. Joseph's in-laws are Egyptian. Joseph's entire world, from age seventeen to age thirty-seven, has been Egyptian. But after some twenty years away from home, he finally has a chance to make a clear declaration of his identity and allegiance! Moreover, the particular names give an even clearer message.

Manasseh

"Joseph called the name of the firstborn Manasseh" (Gen. 41:51). *Manasseh* means *forget*. Joseph fleshes out the meaning of the name of his firstborn when he says, "For . . . God has made me forget all my hardship and all my father's house." Joseph's point here is not that he has forgotten his father, or the covenant community, for that matter. What he means is he has forgotten the hardship. Joseph has chosen to be defined not by the difficulties of his past, but by the promise that gives him hope for his future.

Joseph's choice of this name is a tremendous picture of grace. God alone can be credited with keeping a seventeen-year-old, who experienced all that Joseph did, from becoming a thirty-seven-year-old filled with bitterness, resentment, and hatred toward those who had inflicted hardship upon him.

Choosing the name *Manasseh* is also a picture of the grace that Joseph extended to his brothers. For him to give his son a Hebrew name was to essentially identify the boy with the band of murderous men who had sold him into slavery. Remember, there was no "nation" of Israel at this time. There was just a small clan, most of whom threw Joseph in the pit.

Finally, choosing a Hebrew name for his son is an act of grace toward Manasseh. Joseph was married to the daughter of a pagan priest. He had not been exposed to the worship of Yahweh for two decades.

However, rather than adopt the empty religion and identity of Egypt, and pass that along to his son, Joseph gave him a name that would remind him all the days of his life that he was part of a covenantal community of servants of the Most High God.

Ephraim

"The name of the second he called Ephraim, 'For God has made me fruitful in the land of my affliction'" (41:52). Joseph went even further in the naming of his second son. The name *Ephraim* means *fruitful*. But Joseph's explanation of why he chose the name says much more. In saying that God made him fruitful in the land of his affliction, Joseph goes beyond identifying with the covenant community—he flat-out rejects Egypt and all it has brought him!

Joseph has the finest clothes, jewels, chariots, houses, and lands at his disposal. He has the best foods the land of the Nile had to offer, the finest entertainment, and more. He is living a life of opulent wealth beyond anything he would have experienced as the son of a shepherd. However, he calls *this* the land of his affliction—not the place where he had been despised, rejected, and abandoned. With this second name, Joseph makes it clear that he is not just giving a nod to his heritage; he is identifying himself as a Hebrew among Egyptians.

Thus, this part of the Joseph narrative—the naming of his sons— touches on two of our key themes: covenant and land. First, he identifies himself with the people of the covenant. Joseph is a Hebrew, a servant of Yahweh. He is not an Egyptian pagan. This is incredible news in light of both the rejection and hardship he experienced and the open-armed acceptance Pharaoh lavished upon him. We see here that Joseph would rather be identified with Israel, the shepherd, than Pharaoh, the king of the world.

Second, Joseph identifies himself with the Land of Promise, not with the land of Egypt. It had to be obvious to Joseph that he was never going home again. By now, he knew that his journey from his father's house to find his brothers was a one-way trip. As such, it would have been understandable for him to resign himself to becoming an Egyptian. He spoke the language, knew the customs, and, by this time, had spent more time in Egypt than anywhere else. For all practical purposes, Joseph *was* an Egyptian. However, in his breast beat the hope of the promise God made to Abraham and confirmed with Isaac and Israel.

The remaining theme, *seed*, will arise later. But there are hints of that theme in the conclusion of chapter 41.

THE SEED

At this point, it is important to remember the first toledot: "These are the generations of the heavens and the earth when they were created, in the day that the LORD God made the earth and the heavens" (Gen. 2:4). As noted earlier, the theme of seed was first applied to the land (1:29) before being applied to the Promised Redeemer (3:15). Thus, it should come as no surprise that God ties both concepts together as the narrative unfolds:

> The seven years of plenty that occurred in the land of Egypt came to an end, and the seven years of famine began to come, as Joseph had said. There was famine in all lands, but in all the land of Egypt there was bread. When all the land of Egypt was famished, the people cried to Pharaoh for bread. Pharaoh said to all the Egyptians, "Go to Joseph. What he says to you, do." (Gen. 41:53–55)

Now the land, from which God promised to provide food through seed-bearing plants, has ceased to produce. In other words, God has halted the seed. As a result, there is famine in the land, and there would be starvation were it not for a Hebrew slave-turned-prisoner whom God had sent to Egypt to interpret Pharaoh's dream. Because of this Hebrew, there *is* seed in spite of the fact that the land has stopped producing. But is that the only reason Joseph has come? To save Egypt?

The answer is found in the concluding paragraph:

> So when the famine had spread over all the land, Joseph opened all the storehouses and sold to the Egyptians, for the famine was severe in the land of Egypt. Moreover, all the earth came to Egypt to Joseph to buy grain, because the famine was severe over all the earth. (Gen. 41:56–57)

Now God's providential plan comes into focus. Twenty years prior to the famine, God, knew that (1) the land would cease to produce, (2) his people would starve without intervention, and (3) Egypt would have resources sufficient to store grain during the plentiful years prior to the famine. Consequently, he first sent a dream to Joseph foreshadowing what he was going to do. He then proceeded to use the murderous hatred of Joseph's brothers and the predilections of Ishmael's descendants to send Joseph to Egypt.

In Egypt, God saw to it that Joseph would land in Potiphar's house, preserved him from adultery, and orchestrated his imprisonment so that he was there to meet and interpret the dreams of the king's baker and cupbearer. All of this occurred so the cupbearer would remember Joseph when God sent Pharaoh a dream he could not interpret. Joseph's ability to interpret Pharaoh's dream would lead to his own exaltation, the preservation of the seed, and the overflow of the granaries. Egypt would become the one place in the world where the covenant people of God could come to buy grain and survive.

In short, God sent Joseph to Egypt not to become rich and powerful, but to preserve the promised seed and ensure the salvation of God's people, both in the short run (Israel/Judah) and in the long run (all those who belong to the Lion of Judah)! Praise be to God! How dare we turn this into a ditty about material wealth!

TAKEAWAYS OF GENESIS 41

How many times have we interpreted Genesis 41 wrongly? I'm almost ashamed to answer that question. My natural tendency to read Scripture like a Hollywood screenplay has led me countless times to either think or teach that the great lessons of Genesis 41 center around the reward of material wealth. Mind you, there is much to be said about Joseph's faithfulness and perseverance. I'm not at all saying that those traits are insignificant. However, what do I learn, or more importantly, teach, when I treat those things as the major takeaways from this text? "Try harder, and God will reward you for your efforts?" My friend, there is a better way.

This World Is the Land of Our Affliction,
No Matter How Good It Gets

The New Testament writers make no mention of Joseph's rise to prominence in Egypt. Instead, they focus on his choice of covenant over convenience. Consider the way Stephen preached the Joseph narrative and see if there is any hint of chapter 41 being the big payoff:

> And the patriarchs, jealous of Joseph, sold him into Egypt; but God was with him and rescued him out of all his afflictions and gave him favor and wisdom before Pharaoh, king of Egypt, who made him ruler over Egypt and over all his household. Now there came a famine throughout all Egypt and Canaan, and great affliction, and our fathers could find no food. But when Jacob heard that there was grain in Egypt, he sent out our fathers on their first visit. And on the second visit Joseph made himself known to his brothers, and Joseph's family became known to Pharaoh. And Joseph sent and summoned Jacob his father and all his kindred, seventy-five persons in all. And Jacob went down into Egypt, and he died, he and our fathers, and they were carried back to Shechem and laid in the tomb that Abraham had bought for a sum of silver from the sons of Hamor in Shechem. (Acts 7:9–16)

This is the most extensive treatment of the Joseph narrative in the entire New Testament. Stephen certainly didn't see elevation to power in Egypt as an end in itself. He clearly saw the broader purpose of God as the key to the story. Moreover, just as the author of Hebrews does, Stephen emphasizes Joseph's rejection of Egypt when, addressing the death of Jacob, he writes, "He died, he and our fathers, and they were carried back to Shechem" (Acts 7:15–16). This, like the reference in Hebrews, shows the significance of choosing to be buried in the Land of Promise as opposed to the land of Egypt.

The fact is, no matter how good things get in this world, it's all Egypt! There will never be enough gold chains, fine linen, praise, adoration, or anything else to satisfy the yearning that God has placed in us. Only his presence in the Land of Promise will satisfy his people. The story of Joseph reminds us to look forward "to the city that has foundations, whose designer and builder is God" (Heb. 11:10).

God's People Are Not Defined by the Difficulties of Their Past

It is impossible to read Genesis 41 without being struck by Joseph's response to his past circumstances. This will become even clearer as the story progresses, but already, in naming his firstborn *Manasseh*, we see that Joseph identifies with the people of God. This is the grace of God at work! Only the assurance that comes from knowing, serving, and hoping in God can explain this response in Joseph, or in any of us.

How can I read Joseph's story and continue to wallow in my hurts, disappointments, and weaknesses? The next time you snap somebody's head off because he made you mad, don't reach for your usual "I'm a redhead" or "I'm a hot-blooded Latin (or Irish, or Black, or [insert your ethnic excuse])." Stop and ask yourself if your ethnic background, hair color, anger-filled home in which you were raised, or any other condition of your upbringing is a sufficient excuse for sin.

God is bigger than your past. That parent, sibling, or teacher who abused you does not define who you are today. That person who hurt, disappointed, rejected, or criticized you repeatedly while you were growing up cannot "make" you something that Christ's blood is insufficient to cover. That church you grew up in, filled with backbiting hypocrites, is no excuse for you to reject God's people today. In short, you need a Manasseh! Don't be defined by the difficulties of your past. Instead, be defined by the hope that is yours in Christ.

Naming Children Is a Gospel Opportunity

As a guy with a family name that doesn't really mean anything, I'm probably more sensitive to this one than the average reader. However, the naming of Joseph's sons is such a pivotal point in the story that it cannot be ignored. It comes right on the heels of Joseph being renamed by Pharaoh, which harkens back to the name changes of Joseph's father and his great-grandfather. As such, it teaches us something about the importance and potential impact of names.

Can you imagine what it was like when Ephraim and Manasseh were old enough for Joseph to explain the meaning of their names to them? What an incredible opportunity! "Boys, I want to tell you about your grandfather and your uncles, and how God brought your daddy to Egypt." He had an opportunity to teach them about God's promise to Abraham to make of him a great nation. He was able to teach them about loss and hope. Moreover, he was able to turn mundane introductions of his children into witnessing opportunities.

LOOKING AHEAD

There are myriad other points that could be made about Genesis 41. However, we must remember our goal. We want to see how the story of Joseph fits in the context of redemptive history. As such, Genesis 41 is a pivotal moment where God's providential purpose for Joseph's difficult circumstances comes into focus. But there is still more to uncover. We will see what happens to Joseph's brothers, and whether they've changed. That is the focus of the next section of the Joseph narrative.

6

EXAMINATION

GENESIS 42

One of the most complicated relationships in my life was my relationship with my father. My father didn't raise me. Instead, my mother, still a teenager, was left to raise me alone. The story is much longer and complicated than space allows. But the bottom line is, it was hard for me to trust my father, especially when I got older and began to have children of my own. I simply could not imagine anything that could make me leave them.

Later in life, my father had a drug problem. This only complicated things. Now, not only was it difficult for me to navigate the boundaries of our relationship in light of our past, it was also difficult to trust him because of his addiction. Would he be able to stay sober? Would he go away to rehab again, and disappear for months? Would he steal from me to buy drugs? Can we trust him around our children? These questions and more made it almost impossible to establish a healthy relationship with my father as an adult.

In time, my father was converted. As I spoke with him, his profession of faith sounded credible. My father had become my brother in Christ, but he still struggled with addiction. I know we've all heard testimonies of people who came to faith in Christ and immediately stopped drinking, smoking, or doing drugs. However, most of those

JOSEPH AND THE GOSPEL OF MANY COLORS

people are exaggerating. Even if they aren't, they are the exception, not the rule. The truth is that most people continue to struggle with addiction long after their conversions.

When my father was sober, he would call and want to reestablish contact with me and my family. He loved his daughter-in-law and his grandchildren. Moreover, he was a *great* grandfather! I absolutely loved seeing him in that role. Nevertheless, when he would have a setback, it was difficult to know when and how to trust him again. Sometimes I wondered if it wouldn't be better just to write him off altogether. He had hurt me, and now I was giving him an opportunity to hurt my wife and children. How much latitude should I give him? How much of a risk should I take?

This, in many ways, is the dilemma facing Joseph in Genesis 42. God, in his providence, has orchestrated events in such a way that over twenty years after that fateful day at Dothan, Joseph is reunited with his brothers. But before the reunion, Moses gives us a glimpse into the brothers' lives. Remember, we haven't seen or heard about them in the narrative covering these two decades (except for the Judah account in chap. 38):

> When Jacob learned that there was grain for sale in Egypt, he said to his sons, "Why do you look at one another?" And he said, "Behold, I have heard that there is grain for sale in Egypt. Go down and buy grain for us there, that we may live and not die." So ten of Joseph's brothers went down to buy grain in Egypt. But Jacob did not send Benjamin, Joseph's brother, with his brothers, for he feared that harm might happen to him. Thus the sons of Israel came to buy among the others who came, for the famine was in the land of Canaan. (Gen. 42:1–5)

We find several clues about the brothers' lives in this short paragraph. We know, for example, that Jacob's now middle-aged sons are still living with and depending on him. Jacob speaks to his sons as though they are still small boys who cannot figure out what to do on their own. They are all grown and have wives and children by this time (they will be referenced later in the narrative). However, Jacob is still very much the family patriarch.

We also know that the famine has affected Jacob's family and caused them to turn toward Egypt. Jacob speaks about the need for grain in terms of life and death. This is no small thing. Enough time has passed for them to have run out of all they had and stand in need of more.

Finally, we know that Jacob held Benjamin close for fear that his brothers would allow harm to come to him—or even harm him themselves. The words of verse 4 ("But Jacob did not send Benjamin, Joseph's brother, with his brothers, for he feared that harm might happen to him") are quite telling. Benjamin represented an extra pair of arms and another donkey, and perhaps by this time he had several sons of his own who could carry grain back from Egypt. However, Jacob's fears weighed more heavily upon him than his hunger did.

In short, what we know of Jacob's family is not promising.

THE LONG-AWAITED MEETING

Finally, after two decades—a stint in slavery, several years in prison, and nearly a decade in Pharaoh's court—Joseph meets his brothers again. There's no fanfare. There's no warning, no dream from God to prepare him. He is simply hard at work one day, and there they are:

> Now Joseph was governor over the land. He was the one who sold to all the people of the land. And Joseph's brothers came and bowed themselves before him with their faces to the ground. Joseph saw his brothers and recognized them, but he treated them like strangers and spoke roughly to them. "Where do you come from?" he said. They said, "From the land of Canaan, to buy food." And Joseph recognized his brothers, but they did not recognize him. And Joseph remembered the dreams that he had dreamed of them. And he said to them, "You are spies; you have come to see the nakedness of the land." They said to him, "No, my lord, your servants have come to buy food. We are all sons of one man. We are honest men. Your servants have never been spies." (Gen. 42:6–11)

Did you see it? This is the moment God foretold in Joseph's dream: "And behold, your sheaves gathered around it and bowed down to my sheaf" (Gen. 37:7). When the brothers had first heard of Joseph's dream, they were filled with hatred and resentment. Now, as they stand before a powerful "Egyptian" governor, they have no qualms about bowing down.

This reversal of fortune is quite odd. The Land of Promise is bereft of food; the land of Egypt has plenty to spare. The sons of Jacob are bowed down low; this "son" of Pharaoh stands tall and proud. The men whose hearts were filled with bitterness and hatred cannot even recognize the victim of their crimes, while two decades is not enough to remove their faces from Joseph's memory.

Verse 11 is almost laughable. The brothers say, "We are honest men. Your servants have never been spies." This statement practically invites the investigation into their character. One can almost hear an echo in the text: "We may be murderers, kidnappers, adulterers, and liars, but we are certainly no spies." But, in fairness, that was then. The question Joseph (and the reader) needs to have answered is, what kind of men are they now?

THE TEST OF FAITH

Before Joseph reveals himself to his brothers, he examines them. This is important because there are many unanswered questions that may determine how and when he reveals himself. Remember, he may have to reveal himself as their judge. These men could have killed his father and his younger brother just as easily as they had done away with him. It is not a foregone conclusion that Joseph will be reuniting with these men.

Nor is it out of the ordinary to test the deeds of men to discern their allegiance to the God of the covenant:

> Beware of false prophets, who come to you in sheep's clothing but inwardly are ravenous wolves. You will recognize them by their fruits. Are grapes gathered from thornbushes, or figs from thistles? So, every healthy tree bears good fruit, but the diseased tree bears bad fruit. A healthy tree cannot bear bad fruit, nor can a diseased tree bear good fruit. Every tree that does not bear good fruit is cut down and thrown into the fire. Thus you will recognize them by their fruits. (Matt. 7:15–20)

If the brothers say they are "honest men," then there should be evidence of that. In order to discern their spiritual condition, Joseph subjects his brothers to seven tests. Pay close attention to the questions they are asked, the situations into which they are placed, and the challenges they are given. In doing so, you will not only get an idea of the spiritual temperature of Jacob's sons; you may also learn a thing or two about yourself.

Don't just enjoy the ride. This is the Word of God; allow it to do its work. After all, Paul's admonition is clear: "Examine yourselves, to see whether you are in the faith. Test yourselves. Or do you not realize this about yourselves, that Jesus Christ is in you?—unless indeed you fail to meet the test!" (2 Cor. 13:5). And so the tests begin.

Test 1: Is Benjamin Alive?

Joseph knows that his brothers' murderous hatred of him was rooted in ugly sibling rivalry. Joseph was the favorite because he was the son of Jacob's favorite wife, the only woman he truly *wanted* to marry, Rachel. However, Joseph was not Rachel's only son. His brother, Benjamin, was the only child left of Rachel and Jacob's union. Joseph had to know if the boy was alive, or if his brothers had done away with him:

> He said to them, "No, it is the nakedness of the land that you have come to see." And they said, "We, your servants, are twelve brothers, the sons of one man in the land of Canaan, and behold, the youngest is this day with our father, and one is no more." But Joseph said to them, "It is as I said to you. You are spies. By this you shall be tested: by the life of Pharaoh, you shall not go from this place unless your youngest brother comes here." (Gen. 42:12–15)

Can they produce their younger brother? Or will they have to admit that he, too, "is no more"? This first test has a twofold purpose. First, as we have noted, Joseph wants to know whether his brother is alive. He knew precisely why his brothers hated him. He also knew how Jacob felt about his mother, and could easily surmise that Benjamin would become the new target of his affections. Because of what his brothers had done to him, Joseph had every reason to believe that Benjamin was not safe.

Second, if Benjamin *is* alive, Joseph certainly wants to see his closest sibling. The sibling rivalry fostered by Jacob's favoritism would certainly have created an environment in which the brothers were forced to identify themselves in clans: these are Rachel's boys over here; those are Leah's sons over there, etc. Joseph would most certainly have been closest to Benjamin. Moreover, Benjamin was the only one absent on the day Joseph was betrayed.

Test 2: Will Someone Volunteer to Get Benjamin?

"Send one of you, and let him bring your brother, while you remain confined, that your words may be tested, whether there is truth in you. Or else, by the life of Pharaoh, surely you are spies." And he put them all together in custody for three days. (Gen. 42:16–17)

We can learn much from this second test. First, is there a leader of the clan? Who will rise to the occasion and volunteer to face Jacob and ask for permission to bring his *new* favorite son to Egypt? This would speak volumes about the man who stepped forward. The most likely candidate was the oldest son, Reuben.

Second, is there one whom the others will entrust with this task? Leaders don't always have to volunteer themselves. In fact, if a man is truly a leader, all eyes will turn to him when an opportunity requiring leadership arises. Unfortunately, in this case, there is neither a man who will step forward nor one who is looked upon as being the leader, as is evident by the deafening silence.

Test 3: Will Someone Volunteer to Stay?

On the third day Joseph said to them, "Do this and you will live, for I fear God: if you are honest men, let one of your brothers remain confined where you are in custody, and let the rest go and carry grain for the famine of your households, and bring your youngest brother to me. So your words will be verified, and you shall not die." And they did so. (Gen. 42:18–20)

Test 3 is the *real* test. Remember, these men left Joseph in a pit to be sold into slavery in Egypt, then told his father that he was eaten by wild animals. And they did so only after Judah convinced them that killing him would eliminate the possibility of profiting from their crime financially. If one of them shows enough trust in the other nine to volunteer to be left behind in Egypt, it will be obvious that a change has indeed occurred.

Test 4: Will Someone Come for Simeon?

> Then they said to one another, "In truth we are guilty concerning our brother, in that we saw the distress of his soul, when he begged us and we did not listen. That is why this distress has come upon us." And Reuben answered them, "Did I not tell you not to sin against the boy? But you did not listen. So now there comes a reckoning for his blood." They did not know that Joseph understood them, for there was an interpreter between them. Then he turned away from them and wept. And he returned to them and spoke to them. And he took Simeon from them and bound him before their eyes. (Gen. 42:21–24)

This fourth test comes after a heartrending revelation. There is nothing in Genesis 37 about Joseph "begging" his brothers for mercy. However, as the men talk amongst themselves, we are made privy to the sordid details: "We saw the distress of his soul, when he begged us and we did not listen" (42:21). This, coupled with Joseph's tearful response, gives us just a glimpse into the horror of that day.

And don't think Joseph was the only one affected by what happened. His brothers still introduce themselves as "twelve brothers, the sons of one man in the land of Canaan, and behold, the youngest is this day with our father, and *one is no more*" (42:13). They bring up the horror of that day with no prompting from Joseph. These men had not forgotten what they had done, and they never would.

After pulling back the veil on that horrible day, Moses moves immediately to the application of the fourth test—which, by the way, is confirmation of the brothers' failure of the second and third tests. No one has volunteered to go, and no one has volunteered to stay. Eventually, Joseph makes the decision for them by taking Simeon from them and "binding him before their eyes."

In this profound turn of events, the men who've just conversed amongst themselves about the horror they inflicted on their brother must watch as a very similar thing happens to Simeon. They've already alluded to the fact that this has come upon them because of what they did to Joseph. Joseph's actions must have served only to solidify their belief.

Had they been exposed to the New Testament, perhaps Paul's words would have echoed in their ears: "Do nothing from selfish ambition or conceit, but in humility count others more significant than yourselves. Let each of you look not only to his own interests, but also to the interests of others" (Phil. 2:3–4). But they were left only with the memory of a brother whom they had betrayed, and the sinking feeling as they heard his cries over and over in their heads.

And what about Simeon? He was there when they put Joseph in the pit. He knew that the Midianite traders took him off to Egypt. Every step of the journey down to buy grain, he was reminded of his brother who took the trip alone, possibly in chains. Now, here he was, bound and separated from his family in the same land. How must this have affected him?

Test 5: How Will They Respond to the Money?

And Joseph gave orders to fill their bags with grain, and to replace every man's money in his sack, and to give them provisions for the journey. This was done for them.

Then they loaded their donkeys with their grain and departed. And as one of them opened his sack to give his donkey fodder at the lodging place, he saw his money in the mouth of his sack. He said to his brothers, "My money has been put back; here it is in the mouth of my sack!" At this their hearts failed them, and they turned trembling to one another, saying, "What is this that God has done to us?" (Gen. 42:25–28)

The force of that last line is astonishing. "At this their hearts failed them, and they turned trembling to one another, saying, 'What is this that God has done to us?'" Hitchcock never did better (mainly because this has the weight of truth). These were real people in a real moment in history. Remember, they are reeling emotionally. They have all relived the terrible thing they did to their brother. For all they knew, he died in the very place where they've just left Simeon. Now this!

The question is, if they were so astonished, why didn't they turn back to Egypt to return the money? They hadn't made it all the way home yet, and their brother's life was in jeopardy. Would he be punished for their apparent crime? We don't know the answer, but the question is worth raising. The problem will, however, be resolved later. God is going to use this event to shape this band of brothers.

The remaining tests are not given directly by Joseph. They are, however, related to the events he has set in motion. The only way his brothers are going to be able to comply with his commands is by convincing Jacob to send Benjamin with them back to Egypt. It is this reality that leads inevitably to tests 6 and 7.

Test 6: Have They Earned Jacob's Trust?

> As they emptied their sacks, behold, every man's bundle of money was in his sack. And when they and their father saw their bundles of money, they were afraid. And Jacob their father said to them, "You have bereaved me of my children: Joseph is no more, and Simeon is no more, and now you would take Benjamin. All this has come against me." Then Reuben said to his father, "Kill my two sons if I do not bring him back to you. Put him in my hands, and I will bring him back to you." But he said, "My son shall not go down with you, for his brother is dead, and he is the only one left. If harm should happen to him on the journey that you are to make, you would bring down my gray hairs with sorrow to Sheol." (Gen. 42:35–38)

"The father of the righteous will greatly rejoice; he who fathers a wise son will be glad in him" (Prov. 23:24). Would this proverb be true of Jacob? Has he fathered wise sons? Does he rejoice in them greatly? The answer, unfortunately, is a resounding *no*! His response is telling: "You have bereaved me of my children: Joseph is no more, and Simeon is no more, and now you would take Benjamin. All this has come against me" (v. 36). This is not a man who trusts his sons.

Notice that *Jacob actually blames his sons for Joseph's demise.* This is clear evidence that the brothers have failed test 6. Their father does *not* trust them. Of course, Joseph has forced Jacob's hand. Eventually he will have to let Benjamin go, which means that eventually someone will have to step forward and take responsibility for him. In a dramatic exchange, Reuben attempts to be that man, but to no avail. He offers his two sons to be killed in the event that he does not return with Benjamin.

Jacob's response reveals not only his mistrust of his sons, but also remnants of the favoritism that lay at the root of the rivalry: "My son shall not go down with you, for his brother is dead, and he is the only one left. If harm should happen to him on the journey that you are to make, you would bring down my gray hairs with sorrow to Sheol" (v. 38). Perhaps he was not thinking about what he was saying. But his words, in essence, mean that he is willing to sacrifice Simeon rather than take a chance on losing his beloved Benjamin, the last reminder of the woman he loved.

Test 7: Have They Earned Benjamin's Trust?

The final test takes place in silence. In other words, Moses does not answer the question directly. But a close examination of the facts reveals much. Remember, Benjamin is no boy; he is a grown man, probably in his midthirties. This is significant, since we do not hear from him. He does not speak up and say he is willing to go (or not). He does not advocate for his brother Simeon. In short, he sits in silence while his father condemns his second-oldest brother to death on his behalf. This may not be definitive, but I don't think we can mark it off as a pass. Thus, *the brothers have failed every test they are given*, except the first; Benjamin is indeed alive!

Takeaways of Genesis 42

While these seven tests do not relate to us directly, the four categories they cover most certainly do: (1) Do the sins of your past continue to characterize your present? (2) Have you learned to love one another? (3) How will you respond when facing a moral dilemma? and (4) Have those closest to you seen a change?

In many ways, these four categories are very similar to the "tests" of 1 John, summarized in the final chapter:

Everyone who believes that Jesus is the Christ has been born of God, and everyone who loves the Father loves whoever has been born of him. By this we know that we love the children of God, when we love God and obey his commandments. For this is the love of God, that we keep his commandments. And his commandments are not burdensome. For everyone who has been born of God overcomes the world. And this is the victory that has overcome the world—our faith. Who is it that overcomes the world except the one who believes that Jesus is the Son of God? (1 John 5:1–5)

Of course, the tests in Genesis 42 do not include the person and work of Christ, and right belief therein. However, the similarities are clear. The apostle John encourages us throughout his letter to examine ourselves for evidence that our faith in Christ has produced fruit similar to that being tested in Genesis 42.

Do the Sins of Your Past Continue to Characterize Your Present?

The first category (test 1) goes to the heart of true transformation. Though we may not have sold a brother into slavery, each of us has sins in our past that might have characterized us. As Christians, we must constantly ask ourselves whether the sins of our past continue to characterize our present. "Therefore, if anyone is in Christ, he is a new creation. The old has passed away; behold, the new has come" (2 Cor. 5:17).

Joseph's first test would determine whether his brothers had continued in their bitterness and murderous hatred. More specifically, it would show whether God had brought about a change in their lives. This is something every Christian should consider. We all need reminders like those given to the Corinthian church:

Or do you not know that the unrighteous will not inherit the kingdom of God? Do not be deceived: neither the sexually immoral, nor idolaters, nor adulterers, nor men who practice homosexuality, nor thieves, nor the greedy, nor drunkards, nor revilers, nor swindlers will inherit the kingdom of God. And such were some of you. *But you were washed, you were sanctified, you were justified in the name of the Lord Jesus Christ and by the Spirit of our God.* (1 Cor. 6:9–11)

Making such a statement is a direct result of the grace of God at work in one's life.

Have You Learned to Love One Another?

The second category (tests 2, 3, and 4) is similar to the first. However, it gets right to the heart. Joseph is trying to discern whether his brothers have changed in regard to their love for one another. Is there anything more relevant to those of us who know and love Christ? "By this all people will know that you are my disciples, if you have love for one another" (John 13:35). And conversely, "Everyone who hates his brother is a murderer, and you know that no murderer has eternal life abiding in him" (1 John 3:15).

A life that God has changed will be marked by love for others generally and for God's people particularly. It would be as unthinkable for you and me to claim to have been changed by the power of the gospel without showing evidence of loving the brethren as it was for Joseph to believe that his brothers had changed without seeing evidence of their love for each other.

How Will You Respond When Facing a Moral Dilemma?

The next category of testing has to do with the men's character. In placing the money in their sacks, Joseph gives his brothers an opportunity to show integrity, honesty, and good old intestinal fortitude. While it is easy to stand aloof and think of ways in which we would have passed this test, we must not miss the bigger picture, and the opportunity to reflect on our own need of redemption.

We must be wary of being marked as those who "profess to know God, but they deny him by their works. They are detestable, disobedient, unfit for any good work" (Titus 1:16). On the contrary, as the apostle John notes, "If you know that he is righteous, you may be sure that everyone who practices righteousness has been born of him" (1 John

2:29). Our righteous deeds are evidence of God's work in our lives. After all, "it is God who works in you, both to will and to work for his good pleasure" (Phil. 2:13).

Without such evidence, it would be just as wrong for us to claim that God has done a work in our hearts as it would be to claim that Joseph's brothers have experienced a true change by the end of chapter 42. We, too, must "strive for peace with everyone, and for the holiness without which no one will see the Lord" (Heb. 12:14).

Have Those Closest to You Seen a Change?

Joseph's brothers could have claimed life change until they were blue in the face. However, at some point, had that change truly come, there would have been acknowledgment of it by both Jacob and Benjamin. The fact that neither of them is willing to trust this band of sinners is evidence that they have either not been changed, or that the change has not made its way to the surface. In either case, their transformation is not complete.

It is one thing for me to claim that God has changed me; it is quite another for those around me to acknowledge that I have truly changed. You and I are sinners. Moreover, we are self-deceived. We do not see ourselves accurately. Every one of us thinks more of himself than he ought. We are in desperate need of brothers and sisters who will tell us the truth. More importantly, we need to be the kind of people who acknowledge that truth.

If my brothers and sisters in Christ continue to tell me something about myself that I do not see as true and accurate, I must come to a place where I trust the body, looking at me objectively, more than I trust myself, looking at me subjectively. This is especially true when we are dealing with people who know and love us, those who live and serve in close proximity. Praise God for loving Christian spouses, siblings, and even children in whom both the Spirit of God and a willingness to be lovingly honest abide.

LOOKING AHEAD

Chapter 42 ends in what appears to be abject failure and hopelessness. Aside from knowing that Benjamin is alive, we also know that the brothers don't trust each other, Jacob doesn't trust them collectively (and apparently Benjamin doesn't either), there is no leader among them, and they still lack integrity. Not only do we need a chapter 43—we need some hope. Joseph needs some hope! At this point, he may be better off giving them their grain, sending them on their way, and thanking God for delivering him from such a mess.

However, we know that this is not how the story ends. God *is* going to redeem this family. There *will* be a leader. And Joseph *will* be reunited with a transformed family. Things are dark, but there is indeed hope.

7

TRANSFORMATION

GENESIS 43-44

The results of the testing of Joseph's brothers leave much to be desired. Essentially, the brothers have revealed themselves to be miserable failures. Aside from the fact that they have not killed Benjamin, one could argue that they failed every test to some degree. However, by God's merciful providence, the narrative does not end at chapter 42. There is more to the story.

Oddly, chapter 43 begins with the family having eaten all the grain they brought back from Egypt: "Now the famine was severe in the land. And when they had eaten the grain that they had brought from Egypt, their father said to them, 'Go again, buy us a little food'" (Gen. 43:1–2). I say oddly, because they have a brother who has been taken captive in Egypt, and instead of doing everything they could to retrieve him, they apparently just went about their lives. Jacob evidently has not given much serious thought to the fate of his second-born.

THE ELEPHANT IN THE ROOM

God's providence has left this family in an untenable position. They need more grain from Egypt, and there is no way to get it without dealing with the proverbial elephant in the room:

But Judah said to him, "The man solemnly warned us, saying, 'You shall not see my face unless your brother is with you.' If you will send our brother with us, we will go down and buy you food. But if you will not send him, we will not go down, for the man said to us, 'You shall not see my face, unless your brother is with you.'" (Gen. 43:3–5)

Perhaps this is why there has not been much thought given to Simeon's plight. They all had to know that they there wasn't enough grain to last and that they would eventually have to return to Egypt. Nevertheless, their circumstance leads to an important development.

AN UNEXPECTED LEADER EMERGES

And Judah said to Israel his father, "Send the boy with me, and we will arise and go, that we may live and not die, both we and you and also our little ones. I will be a pledge of his safety. From my hand you shall require him. If I do not bring him back to you and set him before you, then let me bear the blame forever. If we had not delayed, we would now have returned twice." (vv. 8–10)

Jacob has been a terrible father. His sons were murderers (see Genesis 34) whose passions were kindled even against one of their own. He had lost one son, the remaining sons were in disarray, he couldn't trust them to take his grown son down to Egypt, and they were caught flat-footed by the famine. However, in chapter 43, things are about to change.

The use of Jacob's covenantal name throughout this chapter is quite telling. God is fulfilling his promise. He is indeed going to make of Israel a great nation. However, up to this point, that promise has appeared to be in jeopardy. Judah is about to emerge as the head of the family and the son of promise. More importantly, under Judah's leadership, the family will become a nation. But up to this point, there has been nothing to indicate Judah's position. In fact, there has been significant evidence to the contrary.

Judah vs. Reuben

Judah is the one who suggested selling Joseph into slavery as opposed to killing him. However, far from being motivated by an appreciation for life, fear of God's law (Gen. 9:6), or love for his brother, Judah's motivation was profit (Gen. 37:26–27). That's not exactly a leadership quality you want in the head of a family and eventual leader of a nation. There is an interesting connection between Reuben and Judah in this regard. In chapter 37, Reuben, like Judah, urges his brothers not to kill Joseph. However, his motive was "that he might rescue him out of their hand to restore him to his father" (37:22). Here, the firstborn acts as the leader of the family. But knowing that Reuben has been stricken of his preeminence due to his incestuous relationship with his stepmother (35:22), we might question his true motives at Dothan. The text does not explore his motive at all, but the comparison with Judah has become more obvious.

Then later in chapter 42, Reuben offers his sons in pledge for Benjamin. This is different from Judah's offer of himself in pledge, so again, we see a contrast. Israel rejects Reuben's offer. Now, one chapter later, Judah offers himself as pledge, and Israel accepts.

The text is not clear why Israel rejected Reuben's offer. Perhaps Reuben's motives weren't pure. Or perhaps he was rejected because of his sin with Bilhah (see Gen. 35:22). Regardless, the parallels with Judah are unmistakable. Reuben should be the leader, but he is disqualified. Now that position has fallen to Judah. But this is not automatic. After Reuben, the next in line, according to birthright, would be Simeon, and then Levi. There has been nothing to this point to indicate that they have been passed over. Perhaps their sin of murder has disqualified them from leading the family. But again, the text does not tell us. And remember, Judah's hands are certainly not clean in regard to sin.

Wayward in Canaan

In addition to his failure at Dothan, Judah has an entire chapter devoted to his waywardness in Canaan (Genesis 38). As noted earlier, some question the very inclusion of the chapter in this part of the narrative at all. However, as Judah rises to prominence among his brothers, the purpose of chapter 38 becomes clear.

103

If Judah is in the line of the Promised Seed, there must be a record of his descendants. Genesis 38 stands as an essential element in the genealogy of the Messiah! Moreover, it is clear that Judah is chosen not because of what he has done, but in spite of it. It is by grace alone that God has called him to lead the new nation.

Hence, Genesis 38 serves as a checkpoint along the road to redemption in Judah's life. It is where he is separated from the rest of the sinners and where the light shines on his particular need of a Savior—a Savior who would be born to him, from him, and for him as a direct result of his sin. In short, chapter 38 is linked inexorably to chapters 43–44 in terms of Judah's role in the future of God's people.

As the leader of the new nation, Judah must first lead his brothers in passing the tests laid out by Joseph.

PASSING THE TESTS (ISRAEL'S AND BENJAMIN'S TRUST)

> Then their father Israel said to them, "If it must be so, then do this: take some of the choice fruits of the land in your bags, and carry a present down to the man, a little balm and a little honey, gum, myrrh, pistachio nuts, and almonds. Take double the money with you. Carry back with you the money that was returned in the mouth of your sacks. Perhaps it was an oversight. Take also your brother, and arise, go again to the man. May God Almighty grant you mercy before the man, and may he send back your other brother and Benjamin. And as for me, if I am bereaved of my children, I am bereaved." (Gen. 43:11–14)

The most significant phrase in this exchange is, "May God Almighty grant you mercy before the man, and may he send back your other brother and Benjamin." Finally, the patriarch is trusting God. It is God who has promised to make him a great nation. And if Benjamin is to return to him, it will be God who brings it to pass. Jacob can hold on to a single son with all his might. However, Israel must have a broader vision than that.

This leads to a succinct, yet poignant statement: "So the men took this present, and they took double the money with them, and Benjamin. They arose and went down to Egypt and stood before Joseph" (Gen. 43:15).

This is it. This is the "moment of truth." This is also the moment at which Joseph knows the answer to three questions. First, Benjamin is indeed alive and well. The men who murdered an entire village, and were about to murder Joseph, have not harmed his only full sibling. This, as we will see, will touch Joseph deeply.

Second, Jacob has come to trust them. Regardless of what it took to bring it about, the patriarch has come to trust his sons with his most precious possession, Benjamin. He did not pack up his mule and come with them to make sure they didn't harm the boy; he sent them alone. This is no small task, since he has suspected all along that they were responsible for what happened to Joseph.

Third, Benjamin has come to trust them. Having lived for over twenty years with the men who sold his brother into slavery, it is unreasonable to think that Benjamin did not at least have suspicions about what happened. No single person is that good a liar; certainly ten persons could not manage any better, since lies become more, not less, difficult to maintain as the circle of liars grows larger.

PASSING THE TESTS (SIMEON AND THE MONEY)

"And when we came to the lodging place we opened our sacks, and there was each man's money in the mouth of his sack, our money in full weight. So we have brought it again with us, and we have brought other money down with us to buy food. We do not know who put our money in our sacks." He replied, "Peace to you, do not be afraid. Your God and the God of your father has put treasure in your sacks for you. I received your money." Then he brought Simeon out to them. And when the man had brought the men into Joseph's house and given them water, and they had washed their feet, and when he had given their donkeys fodder, they prepared the present for Joseph's coming at noon, for they heard that they should eat bread there. (Gen. 43:21–25)

While they should only get half credit for this one—having gone as long as they possibly could before returning for Simeon, and having taken the money home—the bottom line is they came back for him, and brought the money back with them. There is little fanfare in either case. However, it is important that they finally pass these tests.

Although it is easy to think about the issue of the money solely in terms of the men proving themselves to Joseph, it is important to remember that they are also demonstrating their character before the entire Egyptian court. Joseph has servants, interpreters, and other officials around him at all times during their interactions (as is evident each time he becomes emotional and has to excuse himself).

MORE THAN A GAME

> Then Joseph hurried out, for his compassion grew warm for his brother, and he sought a place to weep. And he entered his chamber and wept there. Then he washed his face and came out. And controlling himself he said, "Serve the food." (Gen. 43:30–31)

Lest we think that Joseph's testing of his brothers is merely a mind game, Moses gives us a glimpse at the overwhelming emotion Joseph is feeling. Though there is still much more going on beneath the surface, this little glimpse speaks volumes. Benjamin is the brother who has done Joseph no harm. He is the brother whose love and loyalty he has never had to question. As a result, he is the brother whose circumstances Joseph had pondered with the greatest trepidation.

Moses continues:

> They served him by himself, and them by themselves, and the Egyptians who ate with him by themselves, because the Egyptians could not eat with the Hebrews, for that is an abomination to the Egyptians. And they sat before him, the firstborn according to his birthright and the youngest according to his youth. And the men looked at one another in amazement. Portions were taken to them from Joseph's table, but Benjamin's portion was five times as much as any of theirs. And they drank and were merry with him. (Gen. 43:32–34)

As he has done repeatedly, Moses gives us, and Joseph's brothers, a glimpse at what is to come. Slowly but surely, Joseph is beginning to reveal himself to his brothers. As he sits them in order, they have to wonder whether God has given the Egyptian insight, or whether something else is afoot.

FINAL EXAMINATION

Then he commanded the steward of his house, "Fill the men's sacks with
food, as much as they can carry, and put each man's money in the mouth
of his sack, and put my cup, the silver cup, in the mouth of the sack of the
youngest, with his money for the grain." And he did as Joseph told him.
As soon as the morning was light, the men were sent away with their
donkeys. They had gone only a short distance from the city. Now Joseph
said to his steward, "Up, follow after the men, and when you overtake
them, say to them, 'Why have you repaid evil for good? Is it not from this
that my lord drinks, and by this that he practices divination? You have
done evil in doing this.'" (Gen. 44:1–5)

Chapter 44 opens with another test. But it is not a new test. Joseph
is about to give the brothers an opportunity to pass a test that they had
failed earlier. Moreover, in this test, Joseph will combine most of the
tests from chapter 42 in one fell swoop. It is also the moment at which
the leader of the family will emerge. However, before that happens,
there is an important scene that demonstrates the unity this ordeal has
created in the family:

When he overtook them, he spoke to them these words. They said to him,
"Why does my lord speak such words as these? Far be it from your servants to do such a thing! Behold, the money that we found in the mouths
of our sacks we brought back to you from the land of Canaan. How then
could we steal silver or gold from your lord's house? Whichever of your
servants is found with it shall die, and we also will be my lord's servants."
He said, "Let it be as you say: he who is found with it shall be my servant,
and the rest of you shall be innocent." Then each man quickly lowered
his sack to the ground, and each man opened his sack. And he searched,
beginning with the eldest and ending with the youngest. And the cup was
found in Benjamin's sack. Then they tore their clothes, and every man
loaded his donkey, and they returned to the city. (Gen. 44:6–13)

The unidentified representative speaks words that illustrate the
confidence he has in his brothers. However, little does he know that his
words will have the potential of costing him and his family everything.
Remember, these are not young boys. These are middle-aged men with
families that depend on them. These are shepherds with flocks to be

tended, husbands with wives and children waiting for them to return. When that cup emerges from Benjamin's sack, it is impossible to depict accurately the level of despair they must have felt.

The words, "they tore their clothes, and every man loaded his donkey, and they returned to the city," are incredibly restrained, and understated. In their minds, this was the end of their lives, the end of their clan. This was the end of God's promise to Abraham, Isaac, and Jacob. In a very real sense, they are taking an emotional walk in Joseph's shoes, even if it is only temporary.

JUDAH: SERVANT OF HIS FATHER

> Then Judah went up to him and said, "Oh, my lord, please let your servant speak a word in my lord's ears, and let not your anger burn against your servant, for you are like Pharaoh himself. My lord asked his servants, saying, 'Have you a father, or a brother?' And we said to my lord, 'We have a father, an old man, and a young brother, the child of his old age. His brother is dead, and he alone is left of his mother's children, and his father loves him.' Then you said to your servants, 'Bring him down to me, that I may set my eyes on him.' We said to my lord, 'The boy cannot leave his father, for if he should leave his father, his father would die.' Then you said to your servants, 'Unless your youngest brother comes down with you, you shall not see my face again.'" (Gen. 44:18–23)

After chapter 38, Judah's name is not mentioned again until chapter 43. In that chapter he is mentioned twice. Here in chapter 44, he is mentioned three times. In chapters 43 and 44 the mention of his name is significant. In 43, he is recognized by his father as the leader of the clan. Here in 44, he is recognized by his brothers, and eventually by Joseph, as the leader. This becomes clear in a number of ways, not least of which is his pleading with Joseph for the life of his brother, Benjamin.

In Genesis 37, there was a clear juxtaposition between Joseph and his other brothers in their commitment to their father's desires. There, Joseph demonstrated his unwavering commitment to do his father's will, while his brothers ignored the fact that their father loved Joseph and decided instead to let their hatred of him drive them. Here, a change has come. Judah mentions his father repeatedly, and his concern is obvious.

JUDAH: SUBSTITUTE FOR THE ONE WHOM HIS FATHER LOVES

Now therefore, as soon as I come to your servant my father, and the boy is not with us, then, as his life is bound up in the boy's life, as soon as he sees that the boy is not with us, he will die, and your servants will bring down the gray hairs of your servant our father with sorrow to Sheol. For your servant became a pledge of safety for the boy to my father, saying, "If I do not bring him back to you, then I shall bear the blame before my father all my life." Now therefore, please let your servant remain instead of the boy as a servant to my lord, and let the boy go back with his brothers. For how can I go back to my father if the boy is not with me? I fear to see the evil that would find my father. (Gen. 44:30–34)

The defining moment in Judah's ascension to prominence comes here at the end of chapter 44. It is no wonder that chapter 45 begins with an emotional Joseph who is simply unable to contain himself in light of what he has seen and heard. Three crucial features of Judah's plea show him not only to be the leader of the patriarch's sons, but the forerunner of Christ.

A Pledge to His Father. Judah has made a pledge to his father, and he intends to keep it, even at great cost to himself. He is prepared to lose all—his own family, his home, his freedom—in order to keep his pledge to his father. This is a beautiful picture of the gospel. There are echoes of Judah's greater son, Jesus, who would later say, "I do as the Father has commanded me, so that the world may know that I love the Father" (John 14:31). And this was not mere conjecture.

Unlike Judah, Jesus would actually lay down his life to fulfill his pledge. And in doing so, he would reiterate his pledge: "No one takes it from me, but I lay it down of my own accord. I have authority to lay it down, and I have authority to take it up again. This charge I have received from my Father" (John 10:18).

A Plea to Joseph. Judah takes the weight of the entire situation on his shoulders when he stands as the representative of his brothers before Joseph. Remember, Judah is not the oldest. In fact, he is the fourth-born among his brothers. Thus, he is not standing forth out of an artificial obligation; this is an expression of genuine leadership.

Reuben has attempted to lead twice in the narrative, both times to no avail. Here, however, he is silent. Simeon and Levi, the second- and third-born, respectively, have stepped up in the past in defense of their sister, Dinah, in perhaps the most notorious episode in the family's history (chap. 34). However, they too remain silent. The stage in this instance, and from this moment on, belongs to Judah.

A Pardon for Benjamin. As Judah offers himself as a ransom for his brother, his transformation is complete. He has gone from being the leading voice in the chorus that led to Joseph's exile to being the lone voice surrendering himself and his freedom in order to return Benjamin to his father. Once more, there are echoes of his greater son, Jesus: "Greater love has no one than this, that someone lay down his life for his friends" (John 15:13). And again, "For even the Son of Man came not to be served but to serve, and to give his life as a ransom for many" (Mark 10:45).

This portrait of Judah is nothing short of a spiritual transformation. This is not desperation or fear. Judah has been changed. The Lord has done a work in the son of promise.

TAKEAWAYS OF GENESIS 43–44

The takeaways in these chapters are as obvious as any we've encountered. First, the takeaways are clearer because of the nature of our journey as a whole. Walking through the Joseph story from a redemptive-historical perspective means looking at the characters, events, and circumstances in ways we perhaps never have before. As a result, our senses have been tuned to the bigger picture, the greater narrative.

Second, the nature of Genesis 42 makes it clear what we ought to be looking for as the tension of that chapter is resolved in chapters 43 and 44. We know that the brothers have to earn the trust of Jacob and Benjamin. We know they have to come back for Simeon, and when they do, they have to bring the money that was returned to their sacks. We also know that someone is going to have to step up and prove himself to be a man that can be trusted, and in turn, one who can lead the family. And that's exactly what we've found.

God Has Transformed Israel's Family

The first, foundational, and greatest truth here is that God has transformed the patriarch and his family. As Wayne Grudem has noted, "This theme, that God overrules the wicked intentions of men and women in order to save his people, runs throughout the Old Testament, but perhaps nowhere more explicitly than in the Joseph narrative."[1] Therefore, it should come as no surprise that this is the primary theme at the climax of the narrative.

Certainly, God has used the famine and Joseph's tests. However, apart from the grace of God working in their lives, there would have been no hope for this band of sinners. Their character up to this point was such that they could never have been able to stand before Joseph with their brother Benjamin without God's intervention.

Perhaps the greatest change is the change in Jacob himself. This change is forecast in the use of his covenantal name, Israel, at the beginning of chapter 43. He has been forced into a situation where he has to trust the Lord. His only alternative would have been to go to Egypt himself, but at his age, the round-trip journey would have been arduous. Hence, we read the poignant words: "May God Almighty grant you mercy before the man, and may he send back your other brother and Benjamin." He is no longer just a father picking favorites among his twelve sons; Israel is a patriarch.

Judah Is the Son of Promise

Like Israel, Judah has stepped into his broader covenantal role. He has finally come forth as the head of the family, the one to lead the next generation into the fuller expression of God's promise to the patriarchs. This confirms several things.

First, Judah's ascension confirms our assertion that the Joseph narrative is ultimately not about Joseph. Joseph does not go to Egypt in order to be set apart as the head of the family. Nor is he identified as the promised seed. Thus, whatever his purpose, it has to be tied to God's broader redemptive plan. As the famine materializes and we see its impact on Israel and his family, it becomes clear why Joseph went to Egypt. However, as Judah emerges as the leader of the family, we see more clearly God's redemptive purpose—specifically, his promise to bring forth a Promised Seed of the woman to conquer the serpent.

Second, Judah's new role explains the placement and prominence of Genesis 38 in the broader narrative. If this story is ultimately about Joseph, the inclusion of Judah's excursion makes no sense. However, if, as the unfolding narrative reveals, Judah is God's choice among his brothers, then the trajectory of his life is an essential part of the Joseph narrative, since he personifies God's redemptive purpose for Joseph.

Finally, the prominence of Judah among his brothers validates his mother, Leah. Leah is not mentioned directly in the Joseph narrative. But without the backstory of Rachel, the woman whom Jacob loved, and the favored children he had with her, Joseph and Benjamin, the sibling rivalry of our narrative would make no sense. Leah was the woman Jacob was tricked into marrying (Gen. 29:24–25). She was his wife of obligation, an unloved (vv. 30–31) and unlovely woman (v. 17), whom he never really wanted. Nevertheless, she is the mother of the son of promise!

Thus, we learn that Jacob's story is no more a love story than Joseph's story is a lesson in revenge. Jacob's story is one of seed, land, and covenant, and Joseph's story is merely one very important chapter in that story.

God's Providence Has Not Failed

Here stands the dysfunctional band of brothers, reeking of murder, incest, deceit, and kidnapping. Yet, after all that they have done, God has redeemed them. This is good news on two fronts. First, if God can redeem this clan, he can redeem you and me! Who among us has a track record worse than Reuben, Simeon, Levi, or Judah? The picture of Judah standing forth offering himself as a ransom for Benjamin is a reminder of God's amazing grace.

Second, this work of redemption reminds us that God is at work accomplishing his broader work of redemption. After all, the redemption of this family is significant primarily because of their place in broader redemptive history. God redeems this family in order to preserve the promised seed and bring forth the ultimate Redeemer, Jesus.

This is a reminder to you and me that we serve a great God, and that there is security in having been "predestined according to the purpose of him who works all things according to the counsel of his will" (Eph. 1:11). God has not left the salvation of his people to chance. Nor has he left it to us. God saves sinners because they cannot save themselves. Remember, "It is God who works in you, both to will and to work for his good pleasure" (Phil. 2:13).

LOOKING AHEAD

Chapter 44 is the last cliffhanger before the great reunion. Joseph is about to reveal himself to his brothers at last. As the tension has grown with his brothers, it has also grown in Joseph. He can no longer bear it. There are no more tests, no more questions. Joseph knows all he needs to know. He has seen Benjamin, and now he longs to see Jacob. But first, he must be reunited and reconciled with his brothers. What lies ahead is perhaps the most emotional scene in the Old Testament.

The next chapter is also the place where speculation meets certainty. Thus far, we have been able to piece together clues as to what God, in his providence, is doing. However, we mustn't hang our hat on speculation. It is one thing to be persuaded that God is working toward revealing a particular purpose; it is quite another for him to tell us so. And in the next chapter, he will do just that. God will remove all doubt as to why Joseph has endured the things he has, and why he has reunited the family.

8

REVELATION

GENESIS 45-46

There have been only a few times in my life when I have felt truly overwhelmed with joy. However, I would be ashamed to offer any of them in comparison to the moment described at the beginning of Genesis 45. Joseph's revelation of himself to his brothers is a truly a moment beyond the ability of most mere mortals to comprehend. This is true for several reasons.

First, few people have ever experienced comparable circumstances. Joseph's circumstances are unique because of the intensity of his brothers' resentment, the magnitude of their actions, the severity of the consequences he suffered, and the amount of time he suffered. All of us have been resented; few have actually had people plot to kill them. All of us have had people harm us; few have been sold into slavery or been imprisoned falsely as a result. All of us have had to endure hardship; few of us have had to do so intensely and without relief for decades. And certainly most people who have experienced these things have not experienced them all at once!

Second, few people have ever had more to miss. Joseph was not just sent away from his home and family. Joseph's home was the Land of Promise, and his family was the household of Jacob, son of Isaac, son of Abraham! He was taken away from the man who wrestled with the angel, the heir of the promise to Abraham.

Finally, those few people who *have* experienced comparable circumstances and actually had as much to miss never got it back. We have all heard horror stories. However, this is not essentially a horror story. This is a story of redemption. Joseph's story is set apart not only by his unique circumstances and the magnitude of his loss; his story is unique because he actually gets to come full circle. Joseph gets to face his attackers. Joseph gets to extend forgiveness. Joseph gets to know the purpose behind his circumstances and see it come to fruition. This is the source of Joseph's uncontainable emotion.

JOSEPH REVEALS HIS IDENTITY

> Then Joseph could not control himself before all those who stood by him. He cried, "Make everyone go out from me." So no one stayed with him when Joseph made himself known to his brothers. And he wept aloud, so that the Egyptians heard it, and the household of Pharaoh heard it. And Joseph said to his brothers, "I am Joseph! Is my father still alive?" But his brothers could not answer him, for they were dismayed at his presence. (Gen. 45:1–3)

Joseph's revelation was not only a surprise to his brothers; it was also a surprise to the Egyptians. He has held the truth close in order not only to test his brothers, but to protect them. Can you imagine what would have happened to them had it been revealed that they were murderous kidnappers who had done harm to a prince of Egypt, a man who has become like a son to Pharaoh? The revelation of Joseph's identity is also a revelation of their identity.

Joseph's brothers are literally speechless. And understandably so. They have just discovered that the brother they thought was dead for more than two decades (essentially at their own hand) is alive. This mysterious Egyptian is not so mysterious anymore. They are truly dismayed.

First, they would have been dismayed that this Egyptian was speaking to them in their own language. Remember, Joseph has used translators up to this point. That is why the brothers talked so freely among themselves in his presence. They had no idea he could understand them. This, in itself, is a very disturbing turn of events.

I once sat on an airport shuttle bus across from a Spanish-speaking couple who were having a very private disagreement in their native tongue. Their disagreement was something best kept for private discussion. However, there were only a few people on the shuttle bus, and none of the rest of us *looked* like we were Hispanic or acted like we understood them. At one point in the discussion, I found myself unable to pretend anymore.

I looked up at them with a "knowing" glance. My Spanish is rusty and my vocabulary limited, but I can usually understand what's going on in a conversation. And, my pronunciation being the last thing to suffer, I tend to speak without an American accent. Upon seeing my glance, this couple instantly knew that I understood what they were saying. The woman asked rather excitedly, "Do you speak Spanish?" "Claro que si (Of course, I do!)!" I responded. When I spoke, she didn't detect an American accent. Now astonished, she asked me, "De donde es? (Where are you from?)" "De aqui en los Estados Unidos. (I'm from right here in America)." Because of my accent, she didn't believe me at first. However, that didn't matter. As the discussion went on, the woman realized her and her husband's indiscretion and was mortified!

As I read Genesis 45:1–3, I think about that woman's face: eyes wide, mouth agape, hand over her mouth. She fell back in her seat and communicated to her husband what had happened without speaking a single word. As they ran through their conversation in their minds, it was as though their nakedness had been exposed. This is precisely where Joseph's brothers found themselves.

Second, they must have been dismayed that they had dealt face-to-face with Joseph for such a long time, and they had never recognized their brother. He had obviously recognized them, but they had absolutely no idea who he was. Of course, this would have to do in part with how young he was when he left. The transformation of a man's body between the ages of seventeen and forty can be an amazing thing. Nevertheless, when they looked into his eyes, his identity would have been unchanged and undeniable. How could they have missed it?

Finally, they would have certainly been dismayed by the horror of their newfound circumstance. They see now that they have been tested.

117

They see now why Benjamin was sought out, then shown favor. They see now why this Egyptian knew their birth order, and why he seemed to be used by God to bring judgment to them for what they had done. At this moment, they would likely have felt great trepidation as they considered what Joseph, now in a position of power and authority, would do to them.

JOSEPH REVEALS HIS THEOLOGY

> So Joseph said to his brothers, "Come near to me, please." And they came near. And he said, "I am your brother, Joseph, whom you sold into Egypt. And now do not be distressed or angry with yourselves because you sold me here, for God sent me before you to preserve life. For the famine has been in the land these two years, and there are yet five years in which there will be neither plowing nor harvest. And God sent me before you to preserve for you a remnant on earth, and to keep alive for you many survivors. So it was not you who sent me here, but God. He has made me a father to Pharaoh, and lord of all his house and ruler over all the land of Egypt. (Gen. 45:4–8)

Here we find one of the most comprehensive examples of the relationship between God's sovereignty and man's freedom. Nor does Joseph attempt to alleviate the tension between these two truths; he just states the facts.

On the one hand, Joseph attributes his brothers' actions to God's sovereign hand. Three times in this brief statement, Joseph refers to God's sovereign work in sending him to Egypt. Joseph tells his brothers, "God sent me before you to preserve life." He then expands on his statement by adding, "God sent me before you to preserve for you a remnant on earth, and to keep alive for you many survivors." And finally, he states, "So it was not you who sent me here, but God." Joseph believes in a sovereign God.

On the other hand, Joseph attributes his brothers' actions to their own wills. In introducing himself, he says, "I am your brother, Joseph, *whom you sold into Egypt.*" In other words, his brothers don't get a pass on their actions simply because the sovereign God used them for his own purposes. God did not force these men to take the actions they did. They did exactly what they intended to do, without the least bit of coercion.

Once again, the Second London Baptist Confession of 1689 is helpful at this point:

> God hath decreed in himself from all eternity, by the most wise and holy counsel of his own will, freely and unchangeably, all things whatsoever comes to pass; yet so as thereby is God neither the author of sin, nor hath fellowship with any therein, nor is violence offered to the will of the Creature, nor yet is the liberty, or contingency of second causes taken away, but rather established, in which appears his wisdom in disposing all things, and power, and faithfulness in accomplishing his decree. (3.1)

"So why would God use sinful men in order to carry out his decree?" If I've been asked this question once, I've been asked a thousand times. And my response is always the same: "Where's God going to find a sinless man to use?" *There are no sinless men!* As Romans 3:23 states: "All have sinned and fall short of the glory of God." Therefore, everything that God does in accomplishing his decree involves sinful men and their sinful actions.

JOSEPH REVEALS HIS PLAN

"Hurry and go up to my father and say to him, 'Thus says your son Joseph, God has made me lord of all Egypt. Come down to me; do not tarry. You shall dwell in the land of Goshen, and you shall be near me, you and your children and your children's children, and your flocks, your herds, and all that you have. There I will provide for you, for there are yet five years of famine to come, so that you and your household, and all that you have, do not come to poverty.' And now your eyes see, and the eyes of my brother Benjamin see, that it is my mouth that speaks to you. You must tell my father of all my honor in Egypt, and of all that you have seen. Hurry and bring my father down here." Then he fell upon his brother Benjamin's neck and wept, and Benjamin wept upon his neck. And he kissed all his brothers and wept upon them. After that his brothers talked with him. (Gen. 45:9–15)

Joseph has thought about this for a long time. He may have been overwhelmed by emotion in the opening scene, but he is not operating out of emotion throughout. He wants to see his father, but he is not driven by that desire. Joseph has a plan. He has considered his family's need and God's provision in the form of his current position ("God has made me lord of all Egypt"), resources ("I will provide for you"), and knowledge ("for there are yet five years of famine to come"). Joseph has seen God's hand in all of this and knows exactly what to do.

GOD REVEALS JOSEPH'S FAVOR WITH PHARAOH

When the report was heard in Pharaoh's house, "Joseph's brothers have come," it pleased Pharaoh and his servants. And Pharaoh said to Joseph, "Say to your brothers, 'Do this: load your beasts and go back to the land of Canaan, and take your father and your households, and come to me, and I will give you the best of the land of Egypt, and you shall eat the fat of the land.' And you, Joseph, are commanded to say, 'Do this: take wagons from the land of Egypt for your little ones and for your wives, and bring your father, and come. Have no concern for your goods, for the best of all the land of Egypt is yours.'" (Gen. 45:16–20)

It is impossible to read this paragraph without seeing the incredible parallel between Israel's entrance into Egypt and their eventual exodus, and between Joseph and Moses. When Israel and his family settle in Egypt, Pharaoh gives Joseph permission to come joyfully; when God's people leave, a later Pharaoh gives Moses permission to go, but grudgingly. When they come to Egypt, Joseph, a Hebrew, is the head of Pharaoh's house; when they leave, Moses, the Hebrew, is one who was raised in Pharaoh's house. When Israel enters Egypt, God uses Joseph's interpretation of dreams to grant him favor with Pharaoh; when they leave, God uses Moses and the plagues to harden Pharaoh.

Moses and Joseph are not the only parallels. When Joseph's family enters Egypt, Pharaoh lavishes wealth upon them to sustain them; when they leave, the Hebrews plunder the Egyptians. When they enter, Pharaoh's chariots escort them on their journey; when they leave, Pharaoh's chariots pursue them. When the people of God enter Egypt, Jacob stops to worship; when they leave, they do the same. When they enter Egypt, God uses disaster to bring them; when they leave, God uses plagues to free them.

But the main distinction has to do with Israel's status. When God's people enter Egypt, they are a small clan—seventy-five people in all, as we shall see. When they leave, God will have literally made them a nation. They will number in the millions! Hence, Egypt is an incubator for the nation of Israel. Their journey is a necessary part of God's plan to grow and multiply them without intermingling them with other nations.

Comparison of the Escape to Egypt and the Exodus

	Entering Egypt	**The Exodus**
Permission	Granted to Joseph by Pharaoh	Granted (reluctantly) to Moses by Pharaoh
Representative	Joseph, head of Pharaoh's house	Moses, raised in Pharaoh's house
Intercession	God gave Joseph favor and softened Pharaoh's heart	God used Moses and the plagues to harden Pharaoh's heart
Wealth	Given by Pharaoh to sustain Jacob on his journey	Plundered from the Egyptians to sustain Israel on their journey
Chariots	Pharaoh sends chariots to retrieve Jacob	Pharaoh sends chariots to destroy Israel
Census	Twelve sons	Twelve tribes
Worship	Jacob stops at a holy place on the way	Moses requests to leave in order that Israel may worship on the Holy Mountain
Disaster	God uses a famine to get Israel to Egypt	God uses plagues to get Israel out of Egypt

THE BROTHERS REVEAL THE TRUTH TO ISRAEL

So they went up out of Egypt and came to the land of Canaan to their father Jacob. And they told him, "Joseph is still alive, and he is ruler over all the land of Egypt." And his heart became numb, for he did not believe them. But when they told him all the words of Joseph, which he had said to them, and when he saw the wagons that Joseph had sent to carry him, the spirit of their father Jacob revived. And Israel said, "It is enough; Joseph my son is still alive. I will go and see him before I die." (Gen. 45:25–28)

Breaking the news to Jacob is almost as emotional as breaking the news to Joseph's brothers. Jacob learns three things that alter his entire world. Jacob receives his son back from the dead. He has been convinced for over two decades that wild animals killed his boy.

He has had to console himself and figure out how to go on with his life having lost the "son of his old age." Like anyone who has lost a loved one, he has had to find a way to honor the memory but move on with his life. Now, out of nowhere, he learns that the boy whom he mourned is still alive! This is almost too much to take in, hence, "his heart became numb."

Jacob learns that God has not only kept his son alive, he has prospered him. Like any father, Jacob wants the best for his children. But he would never have dreamed that Joseph would be "ruler over all the land of Egypt." While Jacob is trusting God to make him a great nation, he lives in a world where Egypt is *the* great nation. Now he hears that his son is ruler there.

Jacob also learns that he is going to see his son before he dies. Certainly it did his heart good to know that his son was alive and prospering. Perhaps that would have been more than enough. However, God, in his mercy, provides a way for Jacob to be reunited with his favorite son before the end of his days. And he doesn't even know the broader redemptive story yet! He still doesn't know about Pharaoh's dream, the five remaining years of famine, and how the Lord used Joseph to save the patriarch and his family.

ISRAEL'S WORSHIP

"So Israel took his journey with all that he had and came to Beersheba, and offered sacrifices to the God of his father Isaac" (Gen. 46:1). With these simple words, Genesis 46 paints a portrait of a transformed patriarch. There is such hope in this brief verse.

First, Jacob is still trusting and obeying God in his old age. We have seen much folly from the son of Isaac. He has been an abominable father. He has refused to listen to God as he spoke to Joseph in dreams reminiscent of those he used to guide Jacob during his tenure with Laban. He has held on to Benjamin with an unhealthy fear. In short, Jacob has not looked like much of a man of God. Then, as though born again by the news of Joseph's well-being, he rises up and demonstrates trust and obedience to God in the midst of his old age.

Second, Jacob knows he is going to Egypt to die, and he makes the journey gladly. He is a feeble old man who is well aware that this is more than likely his last journey. He has watched the promise of God manifest itself in his father's life and in his own. He has held on to the hope that God would make him a great nation and give him the Land of Promise. However, at the end of his life, he sets his sights on the great land to the south, leaving the Land of Promise behind.

Third, Jacob is not holding on to the Promised Land as his own promise in the here and now. If Jacob believed that the land was the quintessential expression of God's promise, he probably wouldn't have left. However, his journey proves that he has a hope that goes beyond the land. Jacob's hope is in a promise greater than mere land. His hope is in the God of promise. Jacob is following God, as was evident by his worship. John Calvin, commenting on this text, offers helpful insight:

> Because the holy man is compelled to leave the land of Canaan and to go elsewhere, he offers, on his departure, a sacrifice to the Lord, for the purpose of testifying that the covenant which God had made with his fathers was confirmed and ratified to himself. For, though he was accustomed to exercise himself in the external worship of God, there was yet a special reason for this sacrifice. And, doubtless, he had then peculiar need of support, lest his faith should fail: for he was about to be deprived of the inheritance promised to him, and of the sight of that land which was the type and the pledge of the heavenly country.[1]

Ultimately, Jacob's hope is in God's faithfulness and the survival of his descendants. Jacob already knows that the promise of God is multigenerational. He is the third in the line of patriarchs. Both Abraham and Isaac were buried in the Land of Promise without seeing the fulfillment of the covenant. Additionally, the nature of the promise—a great nation with descendants as numerous as the stars—is not something that can be fulfilled in a single lifetime or generation. As such, Jacob was not looking to his own day for the fulfillment. Therefore, as he journeyed down to Egypt, he turned his gaze to the God of the covenant and worshiped.

ISRAEL'S GOD REVEALS HIS PRESENCE

And God spoke to Israel in visions of the night and said, "Jacob, Jacob." And he said, "Here I am." Then he said, "I am God, the God of your father. Do not be afraid to go down to Egypt, for there I will make you into a great nation. I myself will go down with you to Egypt, and I will also bring you up again, and Joseph's hand shall close your eyes." (Gen. 46:2–4)

God breaks his long silence. Up to this point, we have had to content ourselves with God's acts of providence. He has been present in the form of his unseen hand. However, we have not heard a direct word. But now, at the most crucial moment in the narrative, the God of Jacob speaks. All of God's people are about to leave the Land of Promise and enter Egypt. The patriarch is leaving the land God promised him. There is a need for God's voice, and he speaks.

God reminds Jacob of his covenant faithfulness. God does not merely identify himself as God. He does not, as in the case of Moses, refer to himself as "I AM." Here, he uses the covenantal identification, "the God of your father." This, coupled with the reiteration of the promise to make Jacob a great nation, serves to remind Jacob of both the past and future of the covenant God made with Abraham. God essentially says to Jacob, "I was faithful to your father, and I am going to be faithful to you." This offers much-needed hope at a crucial moment.

God assures Jacob of his presence. The God who was "with Joseph" in Egypt (Gen. 39:2–3, 21, 23) promises to be with Jacob as well. This ties God's providential work with Joseph with his promise to Jacob. This is especially encouraging in light of the manner in which God has kept Joseph. For Jacob, the fact that the boy is alive and well in Egypt confirms God's faithfulness and gives him hope as he journeys onward. For you and me, it reminds us that God is faithful to his people in the darkest of circumstances.

God reiterates the multigenerational nature of the covenant. There is an odd turn of phrase at the end of God's message to Jacob. On the one hand, he promises him a round-trip journey to Egypt: "I myself will go down with you to Egypt, and I will also bring you up again."

On the other hand, he assures him that Joseph will "close his eyes." In other words, Jacob will die in Egypt, but God will bring Israel out.

This brief message from the Lord is pregnant with meaning. There is no way for Jacob to know the magnitude of his journey. But God does not tell him about hundreds of years of oppression and bondage. He simply tells Jacob that which matters most: "I am God . . . I am in control . . . You can trust me . . . I will bring to pass all that I have promised." This, indeed, is more than enough.

A NATION IN TRANSIT

> Then Jacob set out from Beersheba. The sons of Israel carried Jacob their father, their little ones, and their wives, in the wagons that Pharaoh had sent to carry him. They also took their livestock and their goods, which they had gained in the land of Canaan, and came into Egypt, Jacob and all his offspring with him, his sons, and his sons' sons with him, his daughters, and his sons' daughters. All his offspring he brought with him into Egypt. (Gen. 46:5–7)

Jacob and all his kin came to Egypt. No one stayed behind. This is it—the entire nation of Israel. This is the promise of God in its embryonic phase. They did not leave any of their possessions behind. This is a wholesale move. The great irony, of course, is that Joseph was taken from the Land of Promise decades earlier and has longed for home ever since. Now, instead of him returning to his home, his home is coming to him.

A NATION IDENTIFIED

> All the persons belonging to Jacob who came into Egypt, who were his own descendants, not including Jacob's sons' wives, were sixty-six persons in all. And the sons of Joseph, who were born to him in Egypt, were two. All the persons of the house of Jacob who came into Egypt were seventy. (Gen. 46:26–27)

Chapter 46 ends with a census. After giving the particular genealogies (vv. 8–25), Moses leaves us with a succinct registry of Israel. Seventy souls. Both the genealogies and the final tally are important.

The genealogy is important because of the theme of the promised seed. Since Genesis 3:15, the narrative, and all of redemptive history, has been moving toward God's fulfillment of his promise to our first parents. If this Promised One is to be traced, there must be a careful registry of the people who make up his line. Hence, the genealogies we find throughout the Scriptures serve as a comforting reminder that God is at work fulfilling his promise.

The final tally is important because of the theme of the covenant. Remember, God promised Abraham, "Look toward heaven, and number the stars, if you are able to number them." Then he said to him, "So shall your offspring be" (Gen. 15:5). That promise is being fulfilled. Abraham and Sarah, a couple beyond any hope of having a single heir, now have seventy descendants! And that just two generations later. This is indeed progress. However, it is also a reminder that God is not finished with Israel. Whatever they are walking into in Egypt, it is not the end; it is only the beginning.

TAKEAWAYS OF GENESIS 45–46

There are myriad takeaways in Genesis 45–46. However, if we focus our attention on the broader story of redemption, three things bear mentioning.

A Proper View of God and Man

Joseph's response to his brothers is humble and gracious. There is no hint of gloating or reprisals. Instead he focuses on the more important question: "Why did this happen?" Joseph saw God's sovereign hand in everything that happened. He had no need or desire for revenge. Instead, he was able to acknowledge what had been done to him while focusing primarily on the providential plan that had unfolded. All of this is a byproduct of proper theology (doctrine of God) and anthropology (doctrine of man).

If we understand who God is and who man is, we will avoid a number of errors. Proper theology will keep us from accusing God of evil as he works his plan of redemption in and through our lives. When we find ourselves in prison, or in Potiphar's house, we will be better able to avoid thinking that God's primary job is preventing inconvenience in our lives. Instead, we will acknowledge his sovereignty, providence, and commitment to what is best for his people.

Proper anthropology will keep us from thinking more of man than we ought. We will not attribute power or authority to men that actually belongs to God. We will also be reminded that man is sinful, fallen, and frail. People will fail us, hurt us, disappoint us, and sometimes bless us. However, none of this will happen outside of God's providential plan. Nor will the wicked go unpunished. This is why Paul admonishes, "Beloved, never avenge yourselves, but leave it to the wrath of God, for it is written, 'Vengeance is mine, I will repay, says the Lord'" (Rom. 12:19).

Faith Has No Expiration Date

Seeing the aged patriarch pack up everything he owns and head down to Egypt is both encouraging and humbling. It is easy to think about Christianity as something that gets easier over time. I'll be more stable . . . when I am older. I'll be more mature . . . when I am older. I will have learned all the faith lessons I need . . . when I am older. Jacob's journey reminds us all that we never get to an age where we no longer have to trust God, or where we no longer have lessons to learn, obstacles to overcome, fears to face, sin to mortify, or journeys to take.

Serving God is not a "young man's game" where senior saints sit on the sidelines reminiscing about the good old days. This is a full participation sport, where as long as there is blood coursing through our veins and air in our lungs we must stand at the ready. As Jesus reminds us, "We must work the works of him who sent me while it is day; night is coming, when no one can work" (John 9:4).

God's Promise Probably Won't Be Fulfilled the Way You Expect

Jacob was living in the Land of Promise with his surviving children. He was blessed with dozens of descendants and had the constant reminder of God's covenantal promise in the form of a limp (Gen. 32:25). He had met with God, and there was no reason to doubt that the promises of God were coming to pass. However, he never thought that promise would include taking the promised seed *away* from the promised land for several centuries in order to bring a fully formed nation back into the land. But that's *exactly* what God did.

You and I cannot comprehend God's works, or his ways. "For my thoughts are not your thoughts, neither are your ways my ways, declares the LORD. For as the heavens are higher than the earth, so are my ways higher than your ways and my thoughts than your thoughts" (Isa. 55:8–9). How, then, can we expect him to fulfill his promises through predictable means? If our time in Genesis teaches us anything, it is that God's providence is unpredictable.

Relationships Matter

Throughout our journey, we have traced the theological concepts of seed, land, and covenant, watching God orchestrate events in order to accomplish his plan. However, in Genesis 45–46, we have seen tremendous responses from God's people that had absolutely nothing to do with the depth or breadth of their theological understanding of what was going on.

Joseph was overwhelmed when he revealed himself to his brothers. The brothers were overwhelmed when they learned of Joseph's fate. Jacob was overwhelmed when he discovered that Joseph was alive and prospering. Pharaoh was overwhelmed upon hearing Joseph's news. All of these emotional responses had one thing in common: they were all centered around the importance of relationships.

Certainly the overarching story of God's redemption is important. However, the love of a father, son, brother, or friend is a reality not to be taken for granted. I am grateful to be saved. I am also grateful for relationships with people close to me with whom I can share my journey of redemption. I am grateful that God has not left me to enjoy a sterile, lonely salvation devoid of companionship. Instead, he has placed me in strategic, meaningful relationships that bless me in innumerable ways. Praise God for his common grace!

LOOKING AHEAD

We first look ahead to the next section of the Joseph narrative. We wait anxiously for revelation to give way to reunion as Jacob is reunited with his long-lost son. How will the two of them react? How will the presence of his family alter Joseph's relationship with Pharaoh? How will Israel survive in Egypt? All of these questions and more will not only fill out the narrative, but also give shape to the broader story of redemption.

But we also look ahead to the exodus. Chapters 47–50 in particular have numerous parallels with the exodus. Of course, that story is beyond the scope of this book. However, it is impossible to ignore the relationship between Israel's entrance into Egypt and their eventual departure. Being familiar with the broader redemptive story gives shape, color, and texture to the Joseph story that would otherwise be missed. Having the exodus in mind (and the years in between) helps us raise our eyes above Joseph's circumstances and see something more.

Whether it is the immediate implications and impending reunion, or the broader implications of God's people and their exodus from Egypt, chapters 45–46 drive us forward with anxious anticipation.

9

REUNION

GENESIS 47-48

Chapters 47 and 48 can best be categorized as a story of reunion. Joseph is finally reunited with his entire family. They have come into the land of Egypt and are about to settle and prosper there. The reason for Joseph's hardships is coming into sharper focus, and his family is taking shape. We know that Egypt is not the final stop for the new nation. Hence, chapters 47 and 48 serve an important purpose in the broader narrative.

Chapter 47 is a study in contrasts. Just like chapter 37 gave us a stark contrast between Joseph and his brothers, this chapter does so with Israel and Egypt. First, there is the contrast between Jacob and Pharaoh. Then we see the contrast between the people of Egypt and the people of Israel. Finally, we see the contrast between the land of Egypt and the Land of Promise. The net result of these contrasts is a reminder that Egypt, though prosperous and powerful, has nothing to offer the people of God, especially compared with the promise for which they wait.

RIGHT JOB . . . RIGHT PLACE . . . RIGHT TIME

So Joseph went in and told Pharaoh, "My father and my brothers, with their flocks and herds and all that they possess, have come from the land of Canaan. They are now in the land of Goshen." And from among his brothers he took five men and presented them to Pharaoh. Pharaoh said to his brothers, "What is your occupation?" And they said to Pharaoh, "Your servants are shepherds, as our fathers were." They said to Pharaoh, "We have come to sojourn in the land, for there is no pasture for your servants' flocks, for the famine is severe in the land of Canaan. And now, please let your servants dwell in the land of Goshen." Then Pharaoh said to Joseph, "Your father and your brothers have come to you. The land of Egypt is before you. Settle your father and your brothers in the best of the land. Let them settle in the land of Goshen, and if you know any able men among them, put them in charge of my livestock." (Gen. 47:1–6)

There is an echo here of Joseph's words to his brothers in chapter 46: "When Pharaoh calls you and says, 'What is your occupation?' you shall say, 'Your servants have been keepers of livestock from our youth even until now, both we and our fathers,' in order that you may dwell in the land of Goshen, for every shepherd is an abomination to the Egyptians" (Gen. 46:33–34). His brothers did exactly what he told them to do, and the result was favorable.

However, this passage also creates its own echo. The shepherd theme is prominent in redemptive history. Moses becomes a shepherd in Midian before becoming the shepherd of God's flock (Ex. 3:1). King David was a shepherd. The prophets referred to Israel's leaders as their shepherds. The Savior's birth was announced to shepherds (Luke 2). God refers to himself as a shepherd. And the most cherished image of God in the entire Bible is the image of him as a shepherd in Psalm 23, "The LORD is my shepherd; I shall not want" (v. 1).

Eventually, the shepherd theme finds its culmination in Christ. Jesus is the Good Shepherd who lays down his life for his sheep (John 10:2, 11–12, 14). Ironically, this shepherd is also "the Lamb of God, who takes away the sins of the world!" (John 1:29). Hence, the idea that Israel is set apart because of their role as shepherds is no small thing.

A TALE OF TWO NATIONS

Then Joseph brought in Jacob his father and stood him before Pharaoh, and Jacob blessed Pharaoh. And Pharaoh said to Jacob, "How many are the days of the years of your life?" And Jacob said to Pharaoh, "The days of the years of my sojourning are 130 years. Few and evil have been the days of the years of my life, and they have not attained to the days of the years of the life of my fathers in the days of their sojourning." And Jacob blessed Pharaoh and went out from the presence of Pharaoh. Then Joseph settled his father and his brothers and gave them a possession in the land of Egypt, in the best of the land, in the land of Rameses, as Pharaoh had commanded. And Joseph provided his father, his brothers, and all his father's household with food, according to the number of their dependents. (Gen. 47:7–12)

There's just something about men in power. I have a picture in my office of me standing with then-governor George W. Bush. I have had numerous people come in, look at it, then do a double-take as they realize it's a picture of me standing with the man who was at one time the "leader of the free world." At that point, it doesn't matter what their politics are, they all have the same reaction: "Wow, that is cool." I've gotten that response from conservatives, libertarians, and progressives. There's an awkward sort of "I'm standing next to the man who stood next to the man" response.

Here, Jacob—a simple shepherd, the leader of a clan of seventy sojourners who just left their homeland for fear of starvation—is standing face-to-face with the "leader of the not-so-free world" of his day. But his picture has far more significance than mine. He is standing there as the father of a new nation. Pharaoh would go on to give us pyramids and mummies; Jacob would go on to give us "the commonwealth of Israel . . . the covenants of promise" (Eph. 2:12), and God incarnate.

Moreover, the meeting between the two men sets the stage for the contrast to come. As the narrative unfolds, Egypt declines and Israel prospers.

Egypt's Downward Spiral

Now there was no food in all the land, for the famine was very severe, so that the land of Egypt and the land of Canaan languished by reason of the famine. And Joseph gathered up all the money that was found in the land of Egypt and in the land of Canaan, in exchange for the grain that they bought. And Joseph brought the money into Pharaoh's house. (Gen. 47:13–14)

The narrative of Egypt's downward spiral begins with a rather innocuous statement about Joseph gathering up "all the money that was found in the land of Egypt and in the land of Canaan." What follows is the progressive depletion of the wealth of the Egyptian people and the simultaneous increase in the wealth and power of Pharaoh. There is also a foreshadowing of things to come. Israel will have to deal with the results of this cultural shift generations later in their exodus.

From Money to Livestock

The first phase in this transition from freedom to servitude involves the Egyptians trading their livestock for grain once their money is gone (Gen. 47:15–17). Remember, the sons of Israel are now in charge of Pharaoh's livestock. That means this increase in wealth for Pharaoh would have resulted in an increase in responsibility for Israel.

From Livestock to Land

The next phase in the degradation of the Egyptian people comes when they must trade in their land (Gen. 47:18–19). Their money and livestock are all gone. Their land is not producing. Nevertheless, it is all they possess. This is significant in this context because of the idea of *land* that flows throughout Genesis. Remember, seed, *land*, and covenant. The loss of land by the people of Egypt is a foreshadowing of the heartache that awaits God's people. They have not only left the Land of Promise; they will also suffer under the weight of this same civilization.

From Land to Personal Freedom

At each point, the Egyptian misery has gotten closer to their very persons. First, the Egyptians lost their money. After that, they lost their livestock—a mere commodity certainly, but much more meaningful than money. After losing their livestock, things got even more personal when they lost their land. Now, the only thing left is themselves: "As for the people, he made servants of them from one end of Egypt to the other" (Gen. 47:21). The only ones exempted were the priests, who were already on "a fixed allowance from Pharaoh and lived on the allowance that Pharaoh gave them" (v. 22). Essentially, they were already servants/ property of Pharaoh!

From Personal Freedom to Posterity

The culmination of Egypt's degradation comes in the form of a decree that will confer their indebtedness and servitude to Pharaoh to their children's children:

> Then Joseph said to the people, "Behold, I have this day bought you and your land for Pharaoh. Now here is seed for you, and you shall sow the land. And at the harvests you shall give a fifth to Pharaoh, and four fifths shall be your own, as seed for the field and as food for yourselves and your households, and as food for your little ones." And they said, "You have saved our lives; may it please my lord, we will be servants to Pharaoh." So Joseph made it a statute concerning the land of Egypt, and it stands to this day, that Pharaoh should have the fifth; the land of the priests alone did not become Pharaoh's. (Gen. 47:23–26)

The phrase "your little ones" occurs six times in Genesis; all but one of them occurs in the Joseph narrative (the one exception occurs in Genesis 34 when the brothers wipe out the Shechemites). Use of the phrase here harkens back to the idea of the continuation of the *seed*. In this middle section of chapter 47, the Egyptians have been forced to compromise both *seed* (their little ones) and *land*. Of course, they never did possess the covenant. However, the next section brings that component to bear.

ISRAEL'S PROSPERITY IN EGYPT

> Thus Israel settled in the land of Egypt, in the land of Goshen. And they gained possessions in it, and were fruitful and multiplied greatly. And Jacob lived in the land of Egypt seventeen years. So the days of Jacob, the years of his life, were 147 years. (Gen. 47:27–28)

First, the use of Jacob's covenant name reminds us of the important theme of *covenant*. God has not forgotten his promise to Abraham, Isaac, and Jacob. They are still the covenant people, no matter where they find themselves. The nation is not marked by geopolitical borders, but by people and promise. This was true then, it is true now (Gal. 6:16), and it will be true in eternity in the New Jerusalem (Rev. 3:12; 21:2).

We also learn that "Israel settled in the land of Egypt, in the land of Goshen. And they gained possessions in it." This, of course, brings up a second major theme of the *land*. Granted, this is not the Land of Promise. However, it is significant that Israel gained land and possessions while the Egyptians lost them.

Lastly, we see that Israel began to multiply greatly. This completes the trifecta: *covenant*, *land*, and now *seed*. The contrast could not be clearer. The Joseph narrative hangs on the tension of Joseph's potential loss of seed, land, and covenant. However, he holds on to the covenant as evidenced by the naming of his sons, identifies with the land as evidenced by his view of Egypt as the land of his oppression, and rescues the promised seed, which, as has been revealed, is the ultimate purpose for which he came to Egypt. Now, Israel's plight in Egypt is contrasted directly with that of the Egyptians in these very same areas.

Israel Longs for His Land

> And when the time drew near that Israel must die, he called his son Joseph and said to him, "If now I have found favor in your sight, put your hand under my thigh and promise to deal kindly and truly with me. Do not bury me in Egypt, but let me lie with my fathers. Carry me out of Egypt and bury me in their burying place." He answered, "I will do as you have said." And he said, "Swear to me"; and he swore to him. Then Israel bowed himself upon the head of his bed. (Gen. 47:29–31)

The chapter ends with a reminder that the land in question here is not Egypt. God's promise has not shifted southward. The family does not look upon their newfound favor in the land of Egypt as a sign from God that he has found a better place for them. On the contrary, the patriarch makes it clear, just as Joseph did in chapter 41, that no matter how bad things were in Canaan and no matter how good they appear to be in Egypt, this is not what God has in store for them in the long run.

Israel asks Joseph to place his hand under the patriarch's thigh, a scene reminiscent of Abraham's charge to his servant concerning Isaac's wife. This time, however, the promise has to do with the burial of his bones. This has nothing to do with Israel's superstition; this is about his greater hope. He believes that God is going to make him a great nation, and that that nation will be in the land God promised to his forefathers. This greater hope carries us into Genesis 48. There we find the patriarch at the end of his life embracing his son and grandsons.

Familiar Themes

After this, Joseph was told, "Behold, your father is ill." So he took with him his two sons, Manasseh and Ephraim. And it was told to Jacob, "Your son Joseph has come to you." Then Israel summoned his strength and sat up in bed. And Jacob said to Joseph, "God Almighty appeared to me at Luz in the land of Canaan and blessed me, and said to me, 'Behold, I will make you fruitful and multiply you, and I will make of you a company of peoples and will give this land to your offspring after you for an everlasting possession.' And now your two sons, who were born to you in the land of Egypt before I came to you in Egypt, are mine; Ephraim and Manasseh shall be mine, as Reuben and Simeon are." (Gen. 48:1–5)

Chapter 48 opens with a reiteration of the familiar themes. Joseph is summoned to the side of his dying father. There, his father reminds him of the covenant, which includes a reminder about the land and seed. Additionally, Israel informs Joseph of his intent to adopt Ephraim and Manasseh as his own seed. These themes will be reiterated again and again as we near the end of the Joseph narrative (which is also the end of Genesis).

Israel's recounting of the covenant promise contains the same themes as always. God promises to make him a great nation, to give him innumerable offspring, and to give to that offspring the entire Land of Promise as an everlasting possession. Of course, he has no idea that the promise to which he holds is more intricate than anything he can imagine. However, the fact that he is now in Egypt and not in the Promised Land is more than a hint pointing to his descendants' less-than-ideal future. The greater reality to which the promises point will not come into focus until Christ, the Promised Seed, inaugurates a new and lasting covenant (Jer. 31:31; cf. Luke 22:20; 1 Cor. 11:25; 2 Cor. 3:6; Heb. 8:8, 13; 9:15; 12:24).

Double Take

> When Israel saw Joseph's sons, he said, "Who are these?" Joseph said to his father, "They are my sons, whom God has given me here." And he said, "Bring them to me, please, that I may bless them." Now the eyes of Israel were dim with age, so that he could not see. So Joseph brought them near him, and he kissed them and embraced them. And Israel said to Joseph, "I never expected to see your face; and behold, God has let me see your offspring also." Then Joseph removed them from his knees, and he bowed himself with his face to the earth. And Joseph took them both, Ephraim in his right hand toward Israel's left hand, and Manasseh in his left hand toward Israel's right hand, and brought them near him. And Israel stretched out his right hand and laid it on the head of Ephraim, who was the younger, and his left hand on the head of Manasseh, crossing his hands (for Manasseh was the firstborn). (Gen. 48:8–14)

There is a great deal of irony in this scene. One cannot help but connect this moment to the scene in Genesis 27 when Jacob, taking advantage of his father's age and poor sight, "stole" Esau's blessing from his father, Isaac. Now Jacob's eyes are dimmed with age, and he is at the end of his life. Not only has Jacob assumed the role of dying patriarch, but he has before him a set of brothers. Certainly this moment brought memories of his youthful treachery.

Not only do we see a familiar scene, but we also see a picture of God's redeeming and sanctifying grace. Israel has come full circle. He is no longer Jacob, the "ankle grabber" or a deceiver; he is Israel, the last of the patriarchs! He is not usurping a blessing; he is giving one.

Father of Many Nations

> And he blessed Joseph and said,

> "The God before whom my fathers Abraham and Isaac walked,
>   the God who has been my shepherd all my life long to this day,
> the angel who has redeemed me from all evil, bless the boys;
>   and in them let my name be carried on, and the name of my
>   fathers Abraham and Isaac;
>   and let them grow into a multitude in the midst of the earth."
>   (Gen. 48:15–16)

Remember, Ephraim and Manasseh are the sons of Joseph by an Egyptian woman, just as Ishmael was born of Abraham and an Egyptian woman. However, unlike Ishmael, they are brought into the covenant. Ishmael was indeed blessed, and would become a great nation in his own right. However, in this instance, Ephraim and Manasseh will carry on Israel's name. This is an important distinction, especially for us Gentiles.

Here we see that the covenant is not limited to those descendants "according to the flesh." It is true that "To [the Jews] belong the patriarchs, and from their race, according to the flesh, is the Christ, who is God over all, blessed forever. Amen" (Rom. 9:5). However, we also know that "not all who are descended from Israel belong to Israel" (v. 6), and "if you are Christ's, then you are Abraham's offspring, heirs according to promise" (Gal. 3:29). The adoption of Ephraim and Manasseh are an early glimpse of this truth.

In fact, when John hears the number of those sealed in Revelation 7, he hears a very unusual version of the "twelve tribes of Israel." It is not a list of the twelve land-granted tribes, because Levi is included. Nor is it a list of all the sons, because Dan is excluded. The list does, however, include Joseph and Manasseh. While the full explanation of this anomaly is beyond the scope of our current journey, it is more than appropriate to note that the list of those sealed, and therefore kept through the great tribulation, includes the tribe named for the son of an Egyptian woman. For many, this is an indication of the multiethnic (i.e., Jew/Gentile) nature of the group.

The Older and the Younger

When Joseph saw that his father laid his right hand on the head of Ephraim, it displeased him, and he took his father's hand to move it from Ephraim's head to Manasseh's head. And Joseph said to his father, "Not this way, my father; since this one is the firstborn, put your right hand on his head." But his father refused and said, "I know, my son, I know. He also shall become a people, and he also shall be great. Nevertheless, his younger brother shall be greater than he, and his offspring shall become a multitude of nations." So he blessed them that day, saying,

> "By you Israel will pronounce blessings, saying,
> 'God make you as Ephraim and as Manasseh.'"

Thus he put Ephraim before Manasseh. (Gen. 48:17–20)

The crossing of Israel's hands to bless Ephraim before Manasseh continues another theme prevalent in Genesis. Both Isaac and Jacob were the second sons born to their fathers. Judah, too, was not the firstborn. The subtle message in Genesis is that birth order is not the deciding factor in covenant blessing. The not-so-subtle message in the New Testament is that this is a matter of election and grace, not will and work.

With Ishmael, the message to Abraham—and to us—is that God will accomplish his work without man's aid. With Esau, we learn that even if children are born to the same woman by the same man, God's electing grace does not follow rules like birth order (Romans 9). With Judah, the message is that God will raise up the promised seed from a woman that the patriarch did not choose, love, or even want to marry. It is only fitting that here with Ephraim and Manasseh, Israel crosses his hands and positions the younger before the older.

This is also a beautiful picture of the doctrine of adoption. We, like Ephraim and Manasseh, have been adopted into the covenant family. As a result, we are "pitied, protected, provided for, and chastened by him as by a father, yet never cast off, but sealed to the day of redemption, and inherit the promises as heirs of everlasting salvation" (Second London Baptist Confession, 12).

Restoring Joseph to the Land

> Then Israel said to Joseph, "Behold, I am about to die, but God will be with you and will bring you again to the land of your fathers. Moreover, I have given to you rather than to your brothers one mountain slope that I took from the hand of the Amorites with my sword and with my bow." (Gen. 48:21–22)

Finally, after reiterating the themes of seed and covenant in the blessing of Ephraim and Manasseh, Israel returns to the theme of the land in his closing words to his favorite son, Joseph. Joseph has spent some four decades away from the land of his father's sojourning. Nearly two of those decades have been spent with his family since their reunion. His memories of the land would be faint at best by now. However, his memory of God's promise is vivid because of his father's repeated reminders. As such, his hope, like his father's, is to return to that land.

While Israel's promise is encouraging and true, it is also ironic and a bit sad because Joseph, like Israel, will not return to live in the Land of Promise. He, too, will die in Egypt and have his bones carried back after the exodus. However, once again we are reminded of the greater reality to which the promise points. There is, indeed, a promised land. More specifically, there is a "city that has foundations, whose designer and builder is God" (Heb. 11:10). This is the land to which both Israel and Joseph belong.

TAKEAWAYS OF GENESIS 47–48

Moses uses Genesis 47–48 to summarize and reintroduce several key themes. He also uses the literary tool of juxtaposition to shine light on the most important aspects of the narrative and remind us of where we've been. Therefore, the takeaways in this section are very familiar. In fact, it may be most helpful to concentrate on the three familiar themes of *seed*, *land*, and *covenant* and examine the ways in which they lead us to a redemptive-historical understanding of the broader narrative.

Seed

Both chapters 47 and 48 remind us of the importance of the seed. Chapter 47 gave us the juxtaposition of the people of Egypt, who essentially cursed their seed to servitude to Pharaoh, and Israel, whose seed multiplied and was blessed in the same land. This had nothing to do with the fortitude of Israel's descendants, but was related directly to God's providential protection. Egypt was indeed an incubator for God's people.

Of course, what this means to us, once again, is that God demonstrates his faithfulness to his people, both the immediate nation of

Israel and the eventual Israel of God (Gal. 6:16). God's faithfulness to his people reminds us that we can trust him in the midst of our difficulties. God is not in the business of abandonment. He redeems, transforms, unites, and protects his people. He is indeed a Good Shepherd.

In addition, God's faithfulness to the people whom he will eventually redeem as a result of establishing Israel as a great nation points to the security of our salvation. "For I am sure that neither death nor life, nor angels nor rulers, nor things present nor things to come, nor powers, nor height nor depth, nor anything else in all creation, will be able to separate us from the love of God in Christ Jesus our Lord" (Rom. 8:38–39). Oh, how true this is, particularly in light of God's work in Genesis 47–48!

Land

Even more prevalent than the idea of seed is the idea of *land*. The structure of chapter 47 points again and again to the theme of land. Israel was given the best of the land, and their land prospered. Meanwhile, the Egyptians gave up their land as its barrenness became more overwhelming. But this was only a temporal expression.

The last thought in chapter 47, and one of the prevalent thoughts in 48, is Israel's yearning for his land at the end of his days. He recounts God's covenant blessing concerning the land, makes Joseph swear he will bury him there, and promises Joseph that he will return. Just as we saw with Joseph, no amount of prosperity outside of God's promise was worth as much as the hope, based on God's promises, to which they held.

This is a reminder to all who live and prosper in this land. Regardless of where we find ourselves, no matter how wealthy we become, we all live in the land of our affliction. It's all Egypt! This was one of the takeaways in chapter 41, and we revisit it here because the connection in the text is unmistakable. Israel's opinion of Egypt and the prosperity he has found there is exactly the same as Joseph's. They both long for home! And we should as well.

Covenant

The theme of covenant, though present in both chapters, is much more dominant in chapter 48. There Israel remembers the covenant, reminds Joseph of his place in it, and enfolds Ephraim and Manasseh into the covenant. Joseph's adoption of Ephraim and Manasseh is a clear reminder of that oft-neglected doctrine in the *ordo saludis—adoption*:

> For you did not receive the spirit of slavery to fall back into fear, but you have received the Spirit of adoption as sons, by whom we cry, "Abba! Father!" The Spirit himself bears witness with our spirit that we are children of God, and if children, then heirs—heirs of God and fellow heirs with Christ, provided we suffer with him in order that we may also be glorified with him. (Rom. 8:15–17)

We must take away from the adoption of Ephraim and Manasseh the undeniable, life-changing reality that we are adopted children of the Most High. Moreover, like Ephraim and Manasseh, we are "heirs of God and fellow heirs with Christ." This reality changes the way we view our relationship with God, as well as our relationship with other believers. We are not strangers striving to appease an angry, foreign deity; we are children! We are not striving for acceptance; we are walking in it. This means I do not view my salvation as tenuous, but settled.

Additionally, if we belong to God in this way, we also belong to one another. There are no lone rangers in the body of Christ. Our lives are connected to other believers, "with all humility and gentleness, with patience, bearing with one another in love, eager to maintain the unity of the Spirit in the bond of peace" (Eph. 4:2–3). God is our father and Jesus is our brother, as is every other adopted son and daughter of God. In the words of the familiar hymn:

> Thou our Father, Christ our Brother—
> All who live in love are Thine;
> Teach us how to love each other,
> Lift us to the joy divine.[1]

LOOKING AHEAD

As we turn toward the final two chapters of the Joseph narrative, and the end of the book of Genesis, we do so knowing that Joseph is not the focus. We now see that his story is indeed a branch of Jacob's story. We no longer need to be convinced that Joseph was in Egypt for something more than just revenge. He was there for redemption. Now that the first part of that redemption, the redemption of his family from the famine, has been realized, it is time to turn our attention to the redemption of God's people through the nation he is building and protecting in the incubator of Egypt.

10

RECONCILIATION

GENESIS 49-50

By the end of the story of Joseph's life, two other characters come to overshadow him. Jacob, now Israel, has once again taken center stage in the narrative. However, he is about to take a bow, make his exit, and give way to the new central character, Judah. Judah's role, though, is dominant not because of his words or actions, but because of what is said about him.

Like Frank Miller, the ominous villain in the 1952 classic Western, *High Noon*, Judah actually becomes more intriguing as others describe him than if we were to actually see his actions. Jacob's words paint a picture quite different from what we've seen so far. In fact, he goes beyond describing who Judah has become. He actually gives us a glimpse at what Judah will be. Or more specifically, what will become of his descendants.

But first, Jacob offers blessings, or better yet, condolences, to Judah's three elder brothers. Genesis 49 opens with a familiar scene as Jacob calls the rest of his sons into a meeting similar to what we saw in chapter 27 (stolen blessing) and chapter 48 (Ephraim and Manasseh): "Then Jacob called his sons and said, 'Gather yourselves together, that I may tell you what shall happen to you in days to come. Assemble and listen, O sons of Jacob, listen to Israel your father'" (Gen. 49:1–2). He begins with his firstborn, Reuben.

BLESSED BUT NOT CHOSEN

Reuben, you are my firstborn,
my might, and the firstfruits of my strength,
preeminent in dignity and preeminent in power.
Unstable as water, you shall not have preeminence,
because you went up to your father's bed;
then you defiled it—he went up to my couch! (Gen. 49:3-4)

After the blessing of Ephraim and Manasseh, Jacob's words to Reuben seem harsh and unloving. Nevertheless, they are true. Reuben was guilty of a form of incest, and he lost his place in the family as a direct result (Gen. 35:22). Jacob refers to Reuben's birth order and what should have been true of him as the firstborn, and then gives a reminder of his sin and resulting disqualification.

Simeon and Levi are brothers;
weapons of violence are their swords.
Let my soul come not into their council;
O my glory, be not joined to their company.
For in their anger they killed men,
and in their willfulness they hamstrung oxen.
Cursed be their anger, for it is fierce,
and their wrath, for it is cruel!
I will divide them in Jacob
and scatter them in Israel. (Gen. 49:5-7)

The next two brothers, Simeon and Levi, are the ones who exacted revenge upon the Shechemites (Genesis 34). That is why Jacob says of them, "Weapons of violence are their swords." His words to them end up being even harsher than those he spoke to Reuben: "Cursed be their anger, for it is fierce, and their wrath, for it is cruel! I will divide them in Jacob and scatter them in Israel." This is ironic since Levi's descendants will ultimately occupy the priesthood in the nation of Israel.

JUDAH: THE PROMISED SEED

The point of the first three "blessings" is not so much to lay out the future of the respective sons, but to contrast them with the fourth son, Judah. Judah has distinguished himself already as the *de facto* head of the family. Now, Jacob makes his role more official:

> Judah, your brothers shall praise you;
>> your hand shall be on the neck of your enemies;
>> your father's sons shall bow down before you.
> Judah is a lion's cub;
>> from the prey, my son, you have gone up.
> He stooped down; he crouched as a lion
>> and as a lioness; who dares rouse him?
> The scepter shall not depart from Judah,
>> nor the ruler's staff from between his feet,
> until tribute comes to him;
>> and to him shall be the obedience of the peoples.
> Binding his foal to the vine
>> and his donkey's colt to the choice vine,
> he has washed his garments in wine
>> and his vesture in the blood of grapes.
> His eyes are darker than wine,
>> and his teeth whiter than milk. (Gen. 49:8–12)

The contrast between Judah's blessing and those of his elder brothers is striking. Keil and Delitzsch note that "Judah, the fourth son, was the first to receive a rich and unmixed blessing, the blessing of inalienable supremacy and power."[1] We find four major themes in the blessing that bear further examination.

The Preeminence of Judah

We find Judah's preeminence striking not only when we consider Judah's past, but also when we contrast his blessing with those of all his brothers.

> Jacob's words regarding the remaining sons, with the exception of Joseph, are noticeable, not only for their brevity, but also for their cryptic allusions to epic events that at the time lay yet in the future of the particular tribe. True to the poetic qualities of the text, the images of the destiny of the remaining sons are, in most cases, based on a wordplay of the son's name. The central theme uniting each image is that of prosperity.[2]

The blessing of Judah is, first and foremost, evidence of God's work in Jacob's life (Gen. 37:3–4; 42:35–38). Remember, Jacob picked his favorite from among his sons. More importantly, his choice was based on his feelings about his wives, Rachel and Leah. Judah is a son of Leah, not Rachel. As such, he was not one of the favorite sons. However, Jacob, though his eyes are dim, sees better now than he ever has.

Judah's preeminence is not a result of his own performance. Judah was responsible for Joseph being sold into slavery. Genesis also has an entire chapter devoted to his inappropriate relationship with his daughter-in-law, whom he thought, at the time, was a prostitute (Genesis 38). Clearly, Judah's preeminence is a direct result of God's grace in his life (Gen. 43:9–10; 44:16–34). God has called him to his present post.

The Praise of Judah

In addition to Judah's preeminence, Jacob's words also are full of praise. Jacob offers a play on words with Judah's name—which means "to praise"—just as he does with the rest of his sons. However, in this case, the meaning goes much deeper. This is not a simple play on words. This is the greatest theological truth in redemptive history. This is the promise of the Messiah!

Jacob then states that the nature of Judah's position is praiseworthy. "Your father's sons shall bow down before you" (Gen. 49:8). He is the son of promise. He is the first among his brothers. He is the one to whom they must bow. Judah is essentially taking his father's place.

Additionally, the future of his line is praiseworthy. Judah's line will produce a great king by the name of David. He and his line will rule the nation of Israel, and as such will receive praise from the other tribes. However, the great king David will have a greater Son who will be King of kings. Unlike David, though, this King will be God incarnate and therefore truly worthy of praise.

The Power of Judah

Judah is not only preeminent and praiseworthy, he is also powerful. The picture of a lion illustrates the power of Judah and his descendants. The picture of a lion having killed and eaten, the picture of rest that is only temporary, and the picture of intimidating, awe-inspiring beauty all serve to round out the image of power (Gen. 49:9).

The lion is the most enduring image of Judah in the balance of redemptive history. This image is carried through to the time of the judges, then to the reign of King David, and ultimately is fulfilled in the victorious reign of the Lion of the tribe of Judah, Jesus Christ:

> And one of the elders said to me, "Weep no more; behold, the Lion of the tribe of Judah, the Root of David, has conquered, so that he can open the scroll and its seven seals." . . . And they sang a new song, saying,
>
> > "Worthy are you to take the scroll
> >   and to open its seals,
> > for you were slain, and by your blood you ransomed people for God
> >   from every tribe and language and people and nation,
> > and you have made them a kingdom and priests to our God,
> >   and they shall reign on the earth." (Rev 5:5, 9–10)

The enduring image of the Lion of Judah juxtaposed with the image of the Lamb of God serve as the quintessential images of Christ. Here, though, there is no hint of the lamb; there is only the power of the lion.

In addition to the image of the lion, the picture of the scepter helps round out the idea of Judah's power (v. 10). The lion's power is seen in his stature and strength, while the image of the scepter carries with it the idea of powerful office. Again, the idea of Judah's kingly descendants, and his greater son, Jesus, are in view. Calvin notes, "Though this passage is obscure, it would not have been very difficult to elicit its genuine sense. . . . It is certain that the Messiah, who was to spring from the tribe of Judah, is here promised."[3]

The Prosperity of Judah

Wine, vineyards so plentiful you hitch your donkeys to them, dark eyes, white teeth—all these images point to wealth and prosperity (Gen. 49:11–12). A blessing of prosperity is not unique to Judah. In fact, the theme of prosperity is the most common theme in the rest of Jacob's words to his sons. Nevertheless, the blessing of prosperity to Judah completes the most comprehensive, forward-looking blessing Jacob offers. It also solidifies Judah's place in the line of the Messiah.

If there was any doubt as to upon whom the promise rests, that doubt is removed here in Genesis 49.

The rest of the blessings are significant in their own right. However, for our purposes, ending our discussion with Judah's blessing is sufficient. Suffice to say that Judah's blessing is the only one of significant length and the only one that goes beyond a surface-level play on his name. Which brings us to the summary of the blessings, and the chapter.

JACOB'S RETURN HOME

> All these are the twelve tribes of Israel. This is what their father said to them as he blessed them, blessing each with the blessing suitable to him. Then he commanded them and said to them, "I am to be gathered to my people; bury me with my fathers in the cave that is in the field of Ephron the Hittite, in the cave that is in the field at Machpelah, to the east of Mamre, in the land of Canaan, which Abraham bought with the field from Ephron the Hittite to possess as a burying place. There they buried Abraham and Sarah his wife. There they buried Isaac and Rebekah his wife, and there I buried Leah—the field and the cave that is in it were bought from the Hittites." When Jacob finished commanding his sons, he drew up his feet into the bed and breathed his last and was gathered to his people. (Gen. 49:28–33)

As Jacob comes to the end of his blessings, he also comes to the end of his days. As he does, he reiterates his wish to be buried with the patriarchs. Here he gives a more detailed description of the place, who is buried there, and how it came into their possession. The point is clear: Jacob does not want to remain in Egypt. This, in essence, ends Jacob's last will and testament. He has blessed his sons. He has given his final instructions. He has breathed his last. The patriarch is dead:

> Then Joseph fell on his father's face and wept over him and kissed him. And Joseph commanded his servants the physicians to embalm his father. So the physicians embalmed Israel. Forty days were required for it, for that is how many are required for embalming. And the Egyptians wept for him seventy days. (Gen. 50:1–3)

Jacob's departure from Egypt is filled with significant revelations, one of which is the affection the Egyptians had for the patriarch. Most assuredly, this has to do with Joseph. After all, it was Joseph who saw them through the famine, rescuing Egypt and Canaan. His status would have been legendary. And his father would certainly have been respected and honored as a result.

However, the picture here is not one of respect for Joseph, but of mourning for Jacob. The Egyptians take great care with his remains (a forty-day embalming period) and engage in a prolonged period of mourning. Surely the Egyptians had grown fond of Jacob as well as his son. And the mourning period is followed by an occurrence that, like many events over the past several chapters, has significance when viewed from the perspectives of both the past and the future:

> And when the days of weeping for him were past, Joseph spoke to the household of Pharaoh, saying, "If now I have found favor in your eyes, please speak in the ears of Pharaoh, saying, 'My father made me swear, saying, "I am about to die: in my tomb that I hewed out for myself in the land of Canaan, there shall you bury me."' Now therefore, let me please go up and bury my father. Then I will return." (Gen. 50:4–5)

When viewing this event from the perspective of the past, it is bittersweet. Joseph has been in Egypt for four decades. He entered as a slave in Potiphar's house, then spent several years in prison before ascending to the palace. Nevertheless, in all that time, he was either a slave or a prisoner who could not go home. And by the time he would have earned enough clout to be able to leave, the famine was so bad that his family had to come to him. Now in his fifties or sixties, the man who left home as seventeen is requesting permission to go back.

When viewing this event from the perspective of the future, it is filled with irony. Here Joseph asks Pharaoh for permission to go home, which conjures up pictures of Moses and his requests. And in case you think this is a stretch, remember, Moses is the author of Genesis. He writes this from the perspective of having lived through the exodus!

> And Pharaoh answered, "Go up, and bury your father, as he made you swear." So Joseph went up to bury his father. With him went up all the

151

servants of Pharaoh, the elders of his household, and all the elders of the land of Egypt, as well as all the household of Joseph, his brothers, and his father's household. Only their children, their flocks, and their herds were left in the land of Goshen. And there went up with him both chariots and horsemen. It was a very great company. When they came to the threshing floor of Atad, which is beyond the Jordan, they lamented there with a very great and grievous lamentation, and he made a mourning for his father seven days. (Gen. 50:6–10)

Unlike Moses's experience, Joseph receives an immediate yes, escorts, servants, and resources for the journey. Again, the irony is obvious. This is the anti-exodus. What must have crossed Joseph's mind as he ventured beyond the borders of Egypt? How did it compare to the dreams he must have had in prison or in Potiphar's house? What must the land have looked like to him after all these years? The narrative does not provide answers to any such questions. Remember, this is not about Joseph; this is about Jacob and who will succeed him. Therefore, the focus and perspective have changed. What matters now is getting the patriarch back to his land.

When the inhabitants of the land, the Canaanites, saw the mourning on the threshing floor of Atad, they said, "This is a grievous mourning by the Egyptians." Therefore the place was named Abel-mizraim; it is beyond the Jordan. Thus his sons did for him as he had commanded them, for his sons carried him to the land of Canaan and buried him in the cave of the field at Machpelah, to the east of Mamre, which Abraham bought with the field from Ephron the Hittite to possess as a burying place. After he had buried his father, Joseph returned to Egypt with his brothers and all who had gone up with him to bury his father. (Gen. 50:11–14)

In another twist of irony, Joseph makes the return journey as an obedient son fulfilling the wishes of his father. This is exactly what he was on the day he was sold into slavery. Only this time (1) he has changed direction. He is not going toward his ancestral home but is moving away from it; (2) he has companions. On his previous journey, he was alone. Now he travels with his brothers and a band of Egyptians; (3) he is leading a caravan as opposed to being hauled off by one; (4) his brothers are joining him as he pursues his father's wishes, as opposed to planning to kill him in spite of his father's love for him; and (5) he knows now that he will be seeing his ancestral home for the last time, whereas last time he had no earthly idea.

Nonetheless, this is not the end of the story. Nor is it the end of the strife. There is another page yet to be turned, without which the story cannot end properly.

FORGIVENESS . . . FINALLY

When Joseph's brothers saw that their father was dead, they said, "It may be that Joseph will hate us and pay us back for all the evil that we did to him." So they sent a message to Joseph, saying, "Your father gave this command before he died: 'Say to Joseph, "Please forgive the transgression of your brothers and their sin, because they did evil to you."' And now, please forgive the transgression of the servants of the God of your father." Joseph wept when they spoke to him. His brothers also came and fell down before him and said, "Behold, we are your servants." But Joseph said to them, "Do not fear, for am I in the place of God? As for you, you meant evil against me, but God meant it for good, to bring it about that many people should be kept alive, as they are today. So do not fear; I will provide for you and your little ones." Thus he comforted them and spoke kindly to them. (Gen. 50:15–21)

While Joseph and his brothers have had a reunion, it is not until now that they actually experience reconciliation. Now that their father is dead, Joseph's brothers have a renewed sense of fear and anxiety. In a classic expression of guilt, they reason, "It may be that Joseph will hate us and pay us back for all the evil that we did to him." They expose the fact that they have not reconciled with their brother.

However, their fears are unfounded. Again, Joseph's theology shines through as he responds to his brothers. First, Joseph sees vengeance as God's prerogative, not his own: "Do not fear, for am I in the place of God?" Joseph did not believe that it was his place to punish his brothers for what they had done to him.

Second, Joseph once again clings to the sovereignty and providence of God: "As for you, you meant evil against me, but God meant it for good, to bring it about that many people should be kept alive, as they are today." He could not think about his journey without acknowledging that it was exactly what God intended it to be. Joseph was neither bitter nor angry. Nor was he passive-aggressive. Instead, "he comforted them and spoke kindly to them."

Joseph reconciled with his brothers. He forgave them. He relinquished his right to punish them for what they had done. He cancelled the debt. He was a perfect picture of Paul's words in Ephesians 4, "Let all bitterness and wrath and anger and clamor and slander be put away from you, along with all malice. Be kind to one another, tenderhearted, forgiving one another, as God in Christ forgave you" (Eph. 4:31–32).

THE END OF JOSEPH'S STORY

> So Joseph remained in Egypt, he and his father's house. Joseph lived 110 years. And Joseph saw Ephraim's children of the third generation. The children also of Machir the son of Manasseh were counted as Joseph's own. And Joseph said to his brothers, "I am about to die, but God will visit you and bring you up out of this land to the land that he swore to Abraham, to Isaac, and to Jacob." Then Joseph made the sons of Israel swear, saying, "God will surely visit you, and you shall carry up my bones from here." So Joseph died, being 110 years old. They embalmed him, and he was put in a coffin in Egypt. (Gen. 50:22–26)

Joseph was not the promised seed. Nor was he the central focus of God's redemptive plan in the pages we've examined. However, he was, by God's grace, a child of God who was a picture of faithfulness. As such, God was with him. God was gracious toward him. Nowhere is that more evident than in the final paragraph of the book of Genesis.

Judah has been identified as the son of promise. He was the reason Joseph came to Egypt. He is the one to lead the family, to carry on the line that will culminate in the Messiah. However, in the last paragraph, it is Joseph who stands in the place of the patriarch. In an almost mirror image of the end of Jacob's life, Joseph (1) lives more than a century; (2) is blessed to see his children's children's children; (3) reiterates the covenant promises to his descendants; (4) makes his kinsmen swear to take his bones back to the Land of Promise; and (5) undergoes Egyptian embalming.

After all Joseph has done, it is only fitting that his narrative, and the broader narrative, end this way. Joseph may not have been the promised seed, but he was an heir of the promise. He was a picture of an obedient son who endured undeserved hardship at the hands of wicked kinsmen whom God had sent him to save. Again, this is a very familiar story.

TAKEAWAYS OF GENESIS 49–50

We could take any number of applications from recent chapters and reiterate them here. The narrative has not moved to new places as much as it has brought old ones to a conclusion. However, there are two things in chapters 49–50 that bear mentioning not only because of their prevalence here, but also for their relevance in the broader narrative and the arc of redemptive history. Those two takeaways are forgiveness and hope.

Forgiveness

The most beautiful aspect of this entire narrative is Joseph's ability to forgive. What happened to Joseph was unthinkable. Our natural response is to think that he would have been well within his rights to use his power and position to retaliate against his brothers. However, he does not. He looks to God's sovereignty and trusts his providence. The result is forgiveness. Joseph cancels the debt. That, after all, is what forgiveness means.

Forgiveness does not mean one forgets (as in, has the ability to remember no more) the offense, but that in spite of the memory, one erases the debt. Joseph cannot help but remember what his brothers had done. Retracing his steps on the journey home would have made the memories all the more vivid. In fact, this trip heightens his brothers' sense of guilt and causes them to beg for his mercy. But their debt is gone; it has long since been wiped out. You will not necessarily forget the evil things men do. However, that does not mean you can't or haven't forgiven. You can still cancel the debt and refuse to punish.

If we refuse to forgive, we have stepped into dangerous waters. First, refusing to forgive is to put ourselves in the place of God, as though vengeance were our prerogative, not his. Second, unforgiveness says God's wrath is insufficient. For the unbeliever, we are saying that an eternity in hell is not enough; they need our slap in the face or cold shoulder to "even the scales" of justice. For the believer, we are saying that Christ's humiliation and death are not enough. In other words, we shake our fists at God and say, "Your standards may have been satisfied, but my standard is higher!" Finally, refusing to forgive is the highest form of arrogance. Here we stand forgiven. And as we bask in the forgiveness of a perfectly holy and righteous God, we turn to our brother and say, "My sins are forgivable, but yours are not." In other words, we act as though the sins of others are too significant to forgive while simultaneously believing that ours are not significant enough to matter.

Forgiveness also frees you from the unbearable weight of holding on to an offense. It has been said that holding on to unforgiveness is like drinking poison while hoping the other person dies. When we refuse to forgive others, we give them a level of control over us. Some of us are being controlled by a person who is no longer alive as a direct result of our unwillingness to forgive. We hold the debt close to us like a cherished possession, not realizing that we are in fact the one being possessed. Let it go, friend. If you take nothing else from the story of Joseph, take this: *forgive!*

Hope

Both chapters 49 and 50 end with a death. In chapter 49 the patriarch dies, and in chapter 50 we bid farewell to Joseph. Neither of them lived to see the return to Canaan. As the author of Hebrews points out, "These all died in faith, not having received the things promised, but having seen them and greeted them from afar, and having acknowledged that they were strangers and exiles on the earth" (Heb. 11:13). The message to us is clear. We, too, are "strangers and exiles on the earth."

We, too, will die. Only then will we inherit our full reward. In the meantime, we enjoy the friendship of God, the brotherhood of our fellow Christians, and the pain and heartache of living in the world.

However, as our Savior said, "Take heart; I have overcome the world" (John 16:33).

LOOKING AHEAD

There are no more chapters to cover in Genesis. So we look ahead. In the immediate sense, we look ahead to Exodus. The end of the Joseph narrative is replete with veiled references to the exodus. The relationship between Joseph and Pharaoh, the natural disaster that brought Israel into Goshen, the rapid multiplication of the new nation in the midst of a declining Egyptian culture, and a growing Pharaoh cult all point to what is to come in the book of Exodus. But the closing chapters of Genesis call us even farther afield.

Jacob's blessing of Judah points us ahead to the monarchy and particularly to King David. The echoes of the ruddy shepherd boy who would be king of Israel are so vivid here that they cannot be ignored. In fact, the very division of the kingdom between the ten northern tribes (Israel) and the two southern tribes (Judah) harkens back to these chapters as well.

However, the greater echo calling out from the end of Genesis is the echo of Christ, the Messiah, the Promised Seed. We have caught a glimpse of the Savior to come. He is the Lion of Judah! At the close of Genesis, we can almost hear him roar. No longer are we tempted to limit the Joseph narrative to the story of a boy prospering far away from home. Our attention has been drawn far afield. Joseph is a player in a much more significant drama. God redeems Judah so Judah's son David can be king, and his greater Son, Jesus, can be King of kings, and the Redeemer of God's elect.

Judah offers himself as a substitute for Benjamin, the son whom his father loved. Later, David stands in the valley as a substitute for Israel as he faces Goliath, the representative of the Philistines, the great enemy and oppressor of God's people. Ultimately, Jesus offers himself as a substitute for a people whom his father loved. He goes to a valley, fights and defeats a foe, and redeems a people for his Father. The result is Judah's preeminence, power, prosperity, and praise lavished on the Lion who is the Lamb:

And they sang a new song, saying,

> "Worthy are you to take the scroll
>   and to open its seals,
> for you were slain, and by your blood you ransomed people for God
>   from every tribe and language and people and nation,
> and you have made them a kingdom and priests to our God,
>   and they shall reign on the earth." (Rev. 5:9–10)

Look ahead to the rest of the story of God's redemption. Read the entire Bible in light of the truths we've learned in the story of Joseph. And in every page, look for echoes of the Promised One. He is there. He is always there.

NOTES

Chapter 1: The Lord of the Story

1. Christian Smith, *Soul Searching: The Religious and Spiritual Lives of American Teenagers* (New York: Oxford University Press, 2005).
2. Ibid. See the discussion of Moralistic Therapeutic Deism in chapter 4, pages 118–71.
3. The Bible clearly forbids men in leadership from getting drunk. However, even a cursory reading of texts like Titus ("He must not be arrogant or quick-tempered or a drunkard," 1:7) reveal that an absolute prohibition is unwarranted, and therefore legalistic.
4. Some scholars have even argued that Genesis 38 was misplaced.

Chapter 2: Land, Seed, Covenant

1. Raymond B. Dillard and Tremper Longman, *An Introduction to the Old Testament*, Accordance electronic ed. (Grand Rapids, MI: Zondervan, 1994), 48.
2. Some translations use *offspring* at this point. However, the meaning is the same. Translations that use "seed" as opposed to "offspring" include GENEVA, KJV, ASV, NASB, and HCSB.

Chapter 4: Providence

1. Wayne Grudem, *Systematic Theology: An Introduction to Biblical Doctrine*, Bits & Bytes/Accordance electronic ed. (Grand Rapids, MI: Zondervan, 2008), n.p.
2. Charles Hodge, *Systematic Theology*, Accordance electronic ed. (New York: C. Scribner, 1887), n.p.
3. John H. Walton, "Genesis," in *Genesis, Exodus, Leviticus, Numbers, Deuteronomy*, vol. 1 of Zondervan Illustrated Bible Backgrounds Commentary: Old Testament, ed. John H. Walton, Accordance electronic ed. (Grand Rapids, MI: Zondervan, 2009), 127.
4. Ibid.

Chapter 7: Transformation

1. Wayne Grudem, *Systematic Theology: An Introduction to Biblical Doctrine*, Bits & Bytes/Accordance electronic ed. (Grand Rapids, MI: Zondervan, 2008), n.p.

Chapter 8: Revelation

1. John Calvin, *Genesis*, in Calvin's Commentaries (Complete), trans. John King, Accordance electronic ed. (Edinburgh, UK: Calvin Translation Society, 1847), n.p.

Chapter 9: Reunion

1. "Joyful, Joyful We Adore Thee," Henry van Dyke, 1907.

Chapter 10: Reconciliation

1. C. F. Keil and F. Delitzsch, *Commentary on the Old Testament*, Accordance electronic ed. (Peabody: Hendrickson, 1996), n.p.
2. John H. Sailhamer, *Genesis*, vol. 2 of Expositor's Bible Commentary, eds. Frank E. Gaebelein and J. D. Douglas, Accordance electronic ed. (Grand Rapids, MI: Zondervan, 1990), n.p.
3. John Calvin, *Genesis,* in Calvin's Commentaries (Complete), trans. John King, Accordance electronic ed. (Edinburgh: Calvin Translation Society, 1847), n.p.

RECOMMENDED READING

GENESIS

Bonar, Horatius. *Thoughts on Genesis*. Grand Rapids: Kregel, 1979.

Calvin, John. *A Commentary on Genesis*. London: Banner of Truth, 1965.

Candlish, Robert Smith. *Studies in Genesis*. Grand Rapids: Kregel, 1979.

Dever, Mark. *The Message of the Old Testament: Promises Made*. Wheaton: Crossway, 2006.

Duguid, Ian, and Matthew P. Harmon. *Living in the Light of Inextinguishable Hope: The Gospel According to Joseph*. The Gospel According to the Old Testament. Phillipsburg: P&R, 2013.

Kelly, Douglas F. *Creation and Change: Genesis 1:1–2:4 in the Light of Changing Scientific Paradigms*. Fearn: Mentor, 1997.

Law, Henry. *The Beacons of the Bible: A Series of Tracts*. Weston-super-Mare: Whereat, 1861.

———. *Christ Is All: The Gospel in Genesis*. Edinburgh: Banner of Truth, 1960.

Morris, Henry M. *The Book of Beginnings: A Practical Guide to Understand and Teach Genesis*. Dallas: Institute for Creation Research, 2012.

Pink, Arthur Walkington. *Gleanings in Genesis*. Chicago: Moody, 1922.

CHRIST-CENTERED PREACHING

Chapell, Bryan. *Christ-Centered Preaching: Redeeming the Expository Sermon*. Grand Rapids: Baker, 1994.

Clowney, Edmund P. *Preaching Christ in All of Scripture*. Wheaton: Crossway, 2003.

Goldsworthy, Graeme. *Gospel-Centered Biblical Theology: Hermeneutical Foundations and Principles*. Downers Grove: InterVarsity, 2012.

————. *Gospel-Centered Hermeneutics: Foundations and Principles of Evangelical Biblical Interpretation*. Downers Grove: InterVarsity, 2013.

————. *Preaching the Whole Bible as Christian Scripture: The Application of Biblical Theology to Expository Preaching*. Grand Rapids: Eerdmans, 2000.

Greidanus, Sidney. *Preaching Christ from the Old Testament: A Contemporary Hermeneutical Method*. Grand Rapids: Eerdmans, 1999.

Hendryx, John, ed. *The Sufficiency of Jesus Christ Alone: Classic Essays on the Doctrine of Justification*. Portland: Monergism, 2011. [Digital]

Johnson, Dennis E., *Him We Proclaim: Preaching Christ from All the Scriptures*. Phillipsburg: P&R, 2007.

Mohler, R. Albert. *He Is Not Silent: Preaching in a Postmodern World*. Chicago: Moody, 2008.

Tchividjian, Tullian. *Jesus + Nothing = Everything*. Wheaton: Crossway, 2011.

Thornton, Chipley. "Allegorical Tendencies in Preaching and Their Relation to the Doctrine of the Sufficiency of Scripture." PhD dissertation, The Southern Baptist Theological Seminary, 2009.

GENERAL INDEX

SCRIPTURE INDEX

Also available from
Voddie Baucham

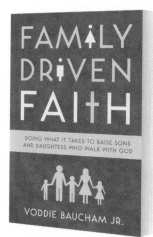
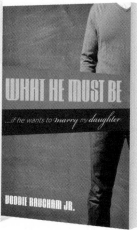
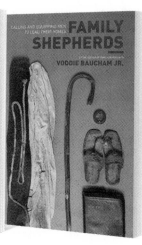

Family Driven Faith equips Christian parents with the tools they need to raise children in a post-Christian, anti-family society. An urgent call to parents to return to biblical discipleship in and through the home.

What will you say when that certain young man sits down in your living room and asks your permission to marry your daughter? *What He Must Be* is a compelling apologetic of biblical manhood, outlining ten qualities parents should look for in a son-in-law.

In *Family Shepherds*, Voddie Baucham teaches men to model and transfer God's truth within their homes, covering topics that span from marriage and parenting to media habits and overcoming difficult family dynamics.